OUR MOON
Has
BLOOD CLOTS

The Exodus of the Kashmiri Pandits

RAHUL PANDITA

RANDOM HOUSE INDIA

First published by Random House India in 2013
Second impression in 2013

Copyright © Rahul Pandita 2013

Random House Publishers India Private Limited
Windsor IT Park, 7th Floor, Tower-B
A-1, Sector-125, Noida-201301 (UP)

Random House Group Limited
20 Vauxhall Bridge Road
London SW1V 2SA
United Kingdom

ISBN: 978-81-8400-087-0

Typeset in Adobe Jenson Pro by SŪRYA, New Delhi

Printed and bound in India by Replika Press Private Limited

Published in association with the New India Foundation

THE ꞰeɯInꝺɪa
FOUNDATION

For Ravi, my brother, my first hero

. . . and an earlier time when the flowers were not stained with blood, the moon with blood clots!
—Pablo Neruda, 'Oh, My Lost City'

The best in me are my memories. Many people will come to life in them, people who gave their blood while they lived, and who will now give their example.
—Anton Donchev, *Time of Parting*

Jammu, 1990

They found the old man dead in his torn tent, with a pack of chilled milk pressed against his right cheek. It was our first June in exile, and the heat felt like a blow in the back of the head. His neighbour, who discovered his lifeless body in the refugee camp, recalled later that he had found his Stewart Warner radio on, playing an old Hindi film song:

> *Aadmi musafir hai*
> *Aata hai, jaata hai*
>
> Man is a traveller
> He comes, he goes

The departed was known to our family. His son and my father were friends. He was born in the Kashmir Valley and had lived along the banks of the Jhelum River.

Triloki Nath was cremated quickly next to the listless waters of the canal in Jammu. Someone remarked that back home the drain next to the old man's house was bigger than the canal. The women of the family were not permitted to wail in his memory. The landlord of the one-room dwelling where Triloki Nath's son lived had been clear: he did not want any mourning noises inside his premises. He said it would bring him bad luck.

It was barely a room. Until a few months ago, it had been a cowshed. Now the floor had been cemented and its walls were painted with cheap blue distemper. The landlord had rented out the room on the condition that no more than four family members could stay there. More people would mean more water consumption. The old man was the fifth member of the family, and that was why he had been forced to live alone in the Muthi refugee camp, set up on the outskirts of Jammu City, on a piece of barren land infested with snakes and scorpions.

Ours was a family of Kashmiri Pandits, and we had fled from Srinagar, in the Kashmir Valley, earlier that year. We had been forced to leave the land where our ancestors had lived for thousands of years. Most of us now sought refuge in the plains of Jammu, because of its proximity to home. I had just turned fourteen, and that June, I lived with my family in a small, damp room in a cheap hotel.

We went to the refugee camp sometimes to meet a friend or a relative. When I went there for the first time, I remember being confronted with the turgid smell of despair emanating from the people who waited for their turns outside latrines, or taps. New families arrived constantly, and they waited at the periphery of the camp for tents to be allotted to them. I saw an old woman wearing her thick pheran in that intense heat, sitting on a bundle and crying. Her son sat nearby mumbling something to himself, a wet towel over his head.

One afternoon I went to the camp to meet a friend. He hadn't turned up at school that day, as his grandmother had fainted that morning from heat and exhaustion. They made her drink glucose water, and she was feeling better now. The two of us went to a corner and sat there on a parapet, talking about girls. We perspired a lot, but in that corner we had a little privacy. Nobody could see us there except a cow that grazed on a patch of comatose grass, and near my feet there was an anthill where ants laboured hard, filling their larder with grains and the wings of a butterfly.

Suddenly there was a commotion, and my friend jumped down and said, 'I think a relief van has come.' While he ran, and I ran after him, he told me that vans came nearly every day, distributing essential items to the camp residents: kerosene oil, biscuits, milk powder, rice, vegetables.

By the time we reached the entrance of the camp, a queue had already formed in front of a load carrier filled with tomatoes. I also stood at the end of it, behind my friend. Two men stood in front of the heap, and one of them gave away a few anaemic tomatoes to the people in the queue. He kept saying, '*Dheere dheere*. Slowly, slowly.' Some people were returning with armfuls of tomatoes. My friend looked at a woman who held them to her breast and he winked at me. Meanwhile, some angry voices rose from the front. The tomatoes were running out, and many people were still waiting. They had begun to give only three tomatoes to each person. In a few minutes it was reduced to one tomato per person. A man in the queue objected to two people from the same family queuing up. 'I have ten mouths to feed,' said one. An old woman intervened. 'Do we have to fight over a few tomatoes now?' she asked. After that, there was silence.

By the time our turn came, and it came in a matter of minutes, it was clear that not everyone would get tomatoes. One of the men distributing them procured a rusty knife. They began to cut the tomatoes into half and give them away. I thought I was hallucinating. Or maybe this was the effect of the hot loo wind that, the inhabitants of this city maintained, could do your head in. I remembered our kitchen garden back home in Srinagar, and all the tomatoes I had wasted, plucking them before they could ripen and hitting them for sixes with my willow bat. And now in my hands somebody had thrust half a tomato. Others in the queue accepted it as I had, and I saw them returning to their tents.

I looked at my friend. There was nothing to say. We returned to our private spot and threw two half slices in front of the cow. We were fourteen. I often think of that moment. Maybe if we had been grown-ups and responsible for our families, we too would have returned silently with those half tomatoes. At fourteen we knew we were refugees, but we had no idea what family meant. And I don't think we realized then that we would never have a home again.

PART ONE

I arrived in Delhi one nippy morning in October 1996 with a rucksack in which I had put two sets of clothes and several books including a well-thumbed copy of Irving Stone's *Lust for Life* that I very nearly knew by heart. The bus that had brought me from Jammu stopped at the Red Fort and suddenly, I felt very vulnerable. I thought this city would suck me into its dark underbelly; it would swallow me whole.

I was one of the thousands of migrants who landed each day at the doorstep of India's capital from every crevice and corner of the country. Like most migrants, I had also come to Delhi in search of a better life, to regain some of what my family had lost during the exodus from the Kashmir Valley. But there was a difference between the other migrants and me. On festivals, and on family functions, or when they were dying, they knew they could go back to where they had come from. I couldn't do that. I knew I was in permanent exile. I could own a house in this city, or any other part of the world, but not in the Kashmir Valley where my family came from.

The sense of vulnerability soon left me as I made friends, and fell in love, and wrote forty-page letters to beloveds until the early hours of the morning, when electric-motor pumps would be switched on in the water-deprived Punjabi colonies inhabited by those who had fled Pakistan after Partition. I ate my first pizza, drank my first whisky. A few years later when my parents joined me after leaving Jammu, I would come home drunk, sometimes way past midnight, and speak in English to my father who would open the door for me. He never spoke to me about it, but when he felt my accent was getting stranger, he would ask my mother to tell me to go easy on the 'Coca-Cola'. That phase is over. I now insist on carrying my own key. But even now, when I come home, my father coughs from inside his room. He won't sleep until I return, whatever the time.

There are no more forty-page letters. All that remains of those days is a plastic bag containing bracelets, photographs with lipstick marks on their backs, and my old copy of *Lust for Life*. There is also an old issue of the *Daily Excelsior* newspaper that every Kashmiri Pandit subscribed to in Jammu because it informed them of who of the community had died in exile. I hardly ever open it. But, sometimes, when I'm angry at the TV shows where our murderers speak about our return, I do. On its front page is a picture of Ravi's mutilated face. The blood from his nose—the result of a blow from the butt of a Kalashnikov—has dried up. His forehead still looks beautiful and clear, and so does his moustache that I had wanted to imitate when I was young.

It is then that the voices come back to me. The loud clapping. The jeering. The chants reaching a crescendo. The hiss of the loudspeaker. The noise beats hard on my chest, like a drumbeat gone berserk. My head feels like an inferno, and a cold sweat traverses down my back.

Hum kya chaaaahte—Azadiiiii!

What do we want—Freeeedom!

Once I was with a few non-Kashmiri friends, and one of them was enacting a scene he had witnessed in video footage shot early in 1990 in Kashmir: a mammoth crowd in Lal Chowk, shouting, 'Indian dogs go back!' and '*Hum kya chahte—Azadi!*'. It made all of them laugh. To me, it brought back memories of the kicks I had braved in school while I sang the National Anthem. But in gatherings like these, my friends shouted for Azadi just for fun. For them it was just a joke—the sight of a crowd clenching fists, demanding freedom in a funny accent. Before I had improved mine, my friends would make fun of me as well.

'Look at our friend here, he doesn't live in *Bharat*, he lives in *Barat*.'

'Tonight, he will go to his *gar*, not *ghar*.'

I would laugh with them, making fun, in turn, of some of them for their inability to use the *nukta*, the small dot that makes *jahaaj* what it is: *jahaaz*.

But this word, Azadi, it frightens me. Images of those days return to haunt me. People out on the roads. People peering out of their windows. People on the rooftops of buses. In shikaras. And in mosques.

'*Hum kya chaaaahte—Azadiiiii!*'

I no longer sing the National Anthem. A few years ago, a child beggar at a traffic signal pinned the national flag onto my shirt. I threw it away in the waste bin of a café near my house.

It was the day I realized I could no longer remember my mother's voice.

When she could still speak, Ma would go for walks in the neighbourhood park in Delhi, wearing her North Star sneakers. Father would watch her close the door quietly behind her and, after she was gone, he would call after her, knowing very well that she could no longer hear him.

'For God's sake, don't repeat your home story in front of everyone!'

The home story was a statement that Ma had got into the habit of telling anyone who would listen. It didn't matter to her whether they cared or not. It had become a part of herself, entrenched like a precious stone in the mosaic of her identity.

By the time her voice had failed her in 2004, I noticed that she had started repeating this statement much too often. But now, when I no longer remember her voice, I realize how much that statement meant to Ma. It was the only thing that reminded her of who she was, more than the occasional glances she would steal at the mirror when no one else was looking.

'Our home in Kashmir had twenty-two rooms.'

I remember the day when I realized I had no memory of her voice. That morning I had been reading the newspapers like I did everyday. I would read a report or two, and Ma would point out advertisements of houses for sale. There were many of them.

'Book now, pay later.'

'Wooden flooring.'

'Uninterrupted power supply.'

'Ten minutes drive from the airport.'

The last one was my mother's favourite. When she could still speak, she would pick up the papers while I was brushing my teeth or shaving, and she would show them to me and say, 'See, this one is close to the airport.'

Ma never got to fly in her life. But she thought proximity to the airport was important to her son.

That morning I sat beside Ma's bed with the papers perched on my lap. I looked at the advertisements for the apartments, then at Ma. Her eyes were open, though hazy with tears that would stream down their corners. Her gaze was fixed at the ceiling above her. The thought crossed my mind that she was counting something; perhaps she was calculating our days and years in exile.

I don't know what happened to me then, I just got up and ran out. I tried to remember how she would comment after sifting through the descriptions of her dream houses. I tried hard. I tried to remember what she would say after discovering flakes of tobacco in the pocket of my white shirt, which she insisted on washing with her own hands. I tried to repeat her voice in my head when she would wake up at midnight after I came home from work or after meeting friends, to serve me piping hot food, curious about how my day had gone. None of it came back to me. No matter how hard I tried, I drew a blank. The words were there, but the texture, tone and contours of her voice had gone missing. They were lost to me forever.

I could not even remember what she sounded like when she chanted what had become her personal anthem for more than a decade: *Our home in Kashmir had twenty-two rooms.*

I remember pressing my foot over a cockroach in desperation as it tried to crawl away.

We don't know for certain where my ancestors originally came from. But in all probability they travelled from the plains of Punjab to settle in the Kashmir Valley, in the lap of the Himalayas, roughly three thousand years ago. They took the same route to enter Kashmir as their future generations took many times to escape from there, mostly due to religious persecution.

The land where they settled had been a lake. The valley had emerged out of this body of water due to a geological event, most probably an earthquake. My ancestors made it home gradually, building a legend around their settlement. They said that the vast lake that Kashmir had been before they settled there was inhabited by a demon called Jalodbhava. He had been granted immortality so long as he remained underwater. It was then that one of our gods drained the lake, sending Jalodbhava into hiding over a hill. Ultimately, our patron goddess assumed the form of a bird and dropped a pebble from her beak that, before landing, turned into a big rock, killing the demon instantly.

The land was abundant with nature's bounty, but geographically isolated. Perhaps under the spell of nature's magnificence, my ancestors took to the pursuit of knowledge. It is thus that Kashmir became the primeval home of the Brahmins, or *Brahmans*—those who are *conscious*.

We developed our own philosophy, our own way of life. We held that the world is real, as opposed to the other Hindu philosophy of the world being *maya*, an illusion. For us, everything in this world was a manifestation of this consciousness. We rejected the otherness of god. We evolved a way of life that was distinct from the bell-ringing, hymn-reciting popular religion. We believed that the world was essentially a creative expression of Shiva, or consciousness. Thus everyone could become Shiva, irrespective of caste or gender.

Kashmir is so beautiful, my grandfather used to say, even the gods are jealous of it. Not only of its beauty, but also of its contribution to art and scholarship. Arthur Anthony MacDonnell, the great professor of Sanskrit at Oxford University, once remarked, 'History is the one weak spot in Indian literature. It is, in fact, non-existent.' But the twelfth-century Kashmiri Pandit scholar, Kalhana, putting aside the Hindu question of existence being 'dream and delusion', penned the magnum opus, *Rajatarangini* (River of Kings), which is counted among the world's most extraordinary historical works.

In the tenth century, the great Kashmiri Pandit scholar Abhinavagupta wrote thirty-five works, including *Tantraloka*, a treatise on Kashmiri Shaivism, and *Abhinavabharti*, a splendid commentary on the *Natyasastra*, the seed of the Indian performing arts. The eleventh century Kashmiri Pandit poet Kshemendra wrote *Brhatkathamanjari*, a collection of stories representing the lost tradition of *brhatkatha* (big story). From the same text, another Pandit scholar, Somadeva, prepared the famous *Kathasaritsagara* (Oceans of the Streams of Stories).

The eleventh century Pandit poet Bilhana had a secret affair with a king's daughter. When it was discovered, he was thrown into prison and ordered to be executed by beheading. Even while facing the prospect of execution, he wrote poetry. It was in the darkness of prison that he wrote his *Chaurapanchasika* (The Collection of Fifty Verses by a Love Thief).

Many centuries earlier, Kashmiri scholars made immense contributions to Buddhism, which came to Kashmir with the emperor Asoka who extended his rule over Kashmir around 250 BC. It was in Kashmir that Buddhist scriptures were written in Sanskrit for the first time. The revered monk Gunavarman, who belonged to a royal family of Kashmir from the fifth century AD, refused the throne when it was offered to him upon the king's death as he had no interest in wordly matters, wishing only to spread the teachings of the Buddha. He travelled to Ceylon, Java and China as well, propagating Buddhism. It was Kumarajiva, a Buddhist monk, whose father was a Kashmiri Pandit, who translated the Buddhist *Lotus Sutra* into Chinese in 406 AD. Guru Padmasambhava, or Rinpoche, who is also referred to as the Second Buddha, spent time in Kashmir, drinking from its knowledge reservoir. A Pandit scholar, Ratnavaja, was assigned the task of rebuilding the circular terrace of the Bsam-yas monastery in central Tibet, which was burnt down in the later part of the tenth century. In the early eleventh century, a female Pandit scholar called Lakshmi travelled to Tibet and taught *Anuttarayoga Tantra*.

It was in the fifth century in Tibet that a Pandit scholar was given the honorary title of *Bhatta*—which means someone who is learned. This name stuck. For the outside world, we were Kashmiri Brahmins or Pandits. But in Kashmir, we remained *Battas*, a derivative of *Bhatta*.

But somehow the gods couldn't make peace with us. So they would wreak upon us disease, earthquakes, floods, famines and fires. And then they gave us rulers susceptible to greed, lust and deceit. And savagery. Fourteen hundred years ago, a ruler called Mihirakula is believed to have been travelling with his army through the Pir Panjal mountain pass when an elephant slipped and fell into a ravine. The cruel king loved the cries of the falling elephant so much that he ordered a hundred elephants to be forced down the mountain.

The two golden phases in Kashmir's history were during the reigns of Lalitaditya and Avantivarman. Lalitaditya ruled Kashmir for about four decades in the early eighth century AD. He was considered a great administrator, and among his achievements the building of the Sun temple at Martand in south Kashmir is considered the greatest. It stands even today in spite of being ravaged by invaders, and is considered one of the most important archaeological sites in India. Of the temple, the British explorer Francis Younghusband wrote:

> The temple is built on the most sublime site occupied by any building in the world—finer far than the site of Parthenon, or of the Taj, or of St. Peters. It is second only to the Egyptians in massiveness and strength and to the Greeks in elegance and grace.

Avantivarman ruled Kashmir for about three decades from 855 AD. Under his rule, the people of Kashmir prospered. He built magnificent temples and Buddhist monasteries and offered patronage to learned scholars.

From the fourteenth century onwards, Islam made inroads into Kashmir. Initially, it fused with local practices and evolved into a way of life rather than a strict, monotheistic religion. There is nothing that reflects this melding more than a *vaakh* by Lal Ded, Kashmir's revered poetess-saint:

> *Shiv chhuy thali'c thali'c rozaan*
> *Mo zaan Hyon'd tey Musalmaan*

> God pervades every particle, every being
> Don't distinguish between a Hindu and a Muslim

But towards the century's end a fanatical ruler called Sultan Sikandar took over the reins of Kashmir and let loose a reign of terror and brutality against his Hindu subjects. He tried to destroy the Martand temple but failed. He imposed taxes on Hindus and forbade them from practising their religion. So much so that he came to be known as *Butshikan*—the idol-breaker. He and his ministers destroyed any Hindu texts they could find. It is said of him that the number of Pandits he murdered was so large that seven maunds of sacred thread worn by them were burnt.

It was during Sikandar's reign that a cry escaped from the lips of the hapless Pandits, to be spared the sword: *Na Bhatto Aham, Na Bhatto Aham!* (I'm not a Pandit, I'm not a Pandit!)

During Sikandar's rule a large number of Islamic scholars flocked to the Valley; many mosques were built and Islam gained influence in Kashmir. Sikandar was succeeded by his son Ali Shah.

After him, his brother Zain-ul-Abidin took over in 1420 AD; he proved to be a tolerant ruler. Legend has it that by this time only eleven Pandit families were left in Kashmir, the majority having either fled or converted to Islam. The historian Srivara, Zain-ul-Abidin's court pandit and musician, described his rule as being, 'like the cooling sandal paste after the harsh summer heat in a desert'. At the insistence of a Pandit physician, Shri Bhatt, the king partially removed religious restrictions on the Pandits. It is believed that the king suffered from a mysterious ailment that nobody could cure and that ultimately, it was Shri Bhatt who cured him. Upon his recovery, Zain-ul-Abidin asked the physician to seek any gift he wanted from him. Shri Bhatt asked that all restrictions imposed upon his fellow Pandits be lifted, and the king readily agreed. He extended an invitation to those Pandits who had fled the Valley to escape Sikandar's wrath. Many of them returned. He appointed many Pandits as his administrators.

Around the late fifteenth century, the Chaks, who were of Dardic descent, came to power. They belonged to the Shia sect of Islam and were intolerant towards both Pandits and Muslims who belonged to the Sunni sect. In 1589, Kashmir was taken over by the Mughals. The Mughal emperor Akbar visited Kashmir that same year. It was during his third visit to Kashmir in 1598 that two Europeans, Father Gerome Xavier and Benoist de Gois, set foot in the Valley for the first time.

Akbar was succeeded by his son Jehangir who, enamoured by Kashmir's natural beauty, built many gardens. At the time of his death in 1627 when Jehangir was asked what he desired, he replied: 'Kashmir, nothing else.'

During Aurangzeb's rule, which lasted for forty-nine years from 1658 onwards, there were many phases during which

Pandits were persecuted. One of his fourteen governors, Iftikhar Khan, who ruled for four years from 1671, was particularly brutal towards the community. It was during his rule that a group of Pandits approached the ninth Sikh Guru, Tegh Bahadur, in Punjab and begged him to save their faith. He told them to return to Kashmir and tell the Mughal rulers that if they could convert him (Tegh Bahadur), all Kashmiri Pandits would accept Islam. This later led to the Guru's martyrdom, but the Pandits were saved.

From 1752 onwards, the Valley slipped into the terrible misfortune of being ruled by Afghans for almost seven decades. In his book *The Valley of Kashmir*, Walter R. Lawrence writes of one of the Afghan governors, Assad Khan:

> It was his practice to tie up the Pandits, two and two, in grass sacks and sink them in the Dal lake. As an amusement, a pitcher filled with ordure would be placed on a Pandit's head and Musalmans would pelt the pitcher with stones till it broke, the unfortunate Hindu being blinded with filth.

During the rule of another governor, Atta Muhammad Khan, Lawrence writes:

> Any Musalman who met a Pandit would jump on his back, and take a ride.

During this tumultuous period, there were mass conversions. The Afghan rulers would surround a group of Pandits with naked swords and ask them to convert. Those who did not comply would be put to death immediately. For the rest, a calf would be slaughtered, and they would be fed its meat and their sacred thread would be snapped.

The troubles at home forced many Pandits to migrate. Many took shelter in Delhi, Lucknow, Lahore and Allahabad, among other places. It was one such family that produced India's first prime minister, Jawaharlal Nehru.

Following the period of Afghan rule, the Valley passed into the hands of Sikh rulers in 1819, and then to the Dogra dynasty, who bought it from the British colonialists for seventy-five lakh rupees, one horse, twelve goats and three cashmere shawls. The Dogra rulers were benevolent towards the Pandits, but treated their Muslim subjects roughly. Many Muslims were forced to work as unpaid labourers. There was widespread discontent and anger towards the Dogra rulers.

That anger also translated into violence against the Pandits.

In 1931, when a Muslim butcher vented his ire against the Dogra Maharaja outside Kashmir's Central Jail, his actions assumed the shape of a riot. A procession then stormed through Srinagar; it torched the Hindu shops in the burgeoning business centre of Maharaj Ganj. As the 'freedom procession' marched on, the crowd stormed into the Vichar Nag area, about nine kilometres from Maharaj Ganj, and recklessly beat up Hindus. Some were killed as well.

In 1947, at a time when the rest of the nation was ravaged with the violence of Partition, Mahatma Gandhi saw the only ray of hope in Kashmir. But he saw that ray in the state's summer capital, Srinagar. In towns bordering Pakistan— Muzaffarabad, Baramulla, Kupwara—the Pandits had to wade through patches of darkness. The last Dogra Maharaja, Hari Singh, was reluctant to join India or Pakistan and wanted to remain independent for as long as possible. In October 1947, Pakistan sent tribal invaders from the Northwest Frontier Province, aided by Pakistani Army regulars, to occupy Kashmir.

In many places, they were aided and guided by Muslims in Kashmir. But at the last moment, when the Valley was about to slip into the hands of the invaders, Maharaja Hari Singh signed the instrument of accession and Kashmir became a part of India. The Indian Army arrived in Srinagar and the tribal invaders were pushed back.

In 1948, the Kashmiri political leader Sheikh Mohammed Abdullah, who had been a strong opponent of Dogra rule in Kashmir, made his pact with India by standing next to Jawaharlal Nehru and reciting a Persian couplet: '*Mann tu shudi, tu mann shudi, Ta kas na goyed, Man degram tu degri.*' (I became you and you became me, so nobody can think of us as separate.)

But this bonhomie was shortlived. The relationship between Sheikh Abdullah and Jawaharlal Nehru soured, and Kashmir and India remained at loggerheads with each other. Later, forgetting how many Pandits had taken an active part in his struggle against the Dogra Maharaja, Sheikh Abdullah would also direct his bitterness towards the Pandits, a community to which his own grandfather belonged, before he converted to Islam. He would tell Pandits: '*Raliv, Chaliv, ya Galiv.*' (Be one among us, flee, or be decimated.)

Srinagar, Early 1980s

Dedda believed that Charlie Chaplin was the Englishman's god. She had a poster of him pinned up on a wall in her room, and sometimes I caught her looking at it with rapt attention, one hand clutching a corner of her muslin sari. Sometimes she would have an argument with a family member and afterwards, she would stand in front of it and mumble—in complaint or prayer, I don't know.

Dedda was my mother's mother. She lived next door with her son's family in a house separated from ours by a dwarf wooden fence. Between the two houses lay our respective kitchen gardens, and I suspect there was some kind of competition between us and my uncle's household. But, overall, it was a level playing field. There were brinjals, collard greens, chillies, radish, pumpkin, bottle gourd, corn, cucumber, knol-khol, and mountain mint. There were fruit trees in the garden as well— an apple tree in ours and an apricot tree in theirs. When I was very young, I remember other fruit trees as well, but they had been cut down before a family wedding to accommodate a giant tent. Our tree produced apples of the sour variety and I remember Dedda plucking one or two on sunny afternoons and then slicing them with her pocketknife, and applying salt over them with girlish delight. It must have given her immense joy and I believe it was her idea of sin—the sour juice gurgling in her mouth, tingling her senses, resulting in her gently scratching her cheeks.

Dedda would get up early and light the fire in her hearth. She always cooked in earthen pots until she became old and her daughter-in-law took over, bringing with her steel and aluminium utensils. Dedda stirred her dishes with a wooden ladle, reciting verses of Lal Ded. She was a magician with everything but I particularly remember her delicious beans and dried turnip, and dried bottle gourd and brinjals.

Often Tathya, my maternal grandfather, brought guests to the house and they invariably stayed for lunch. Tathya would worry that there might not be enough food and he would steal questioning glances at Dedda. She always responded with a smile. She wouldn't allow even a peep inside her vessels. No matter how many guests came, her vessels produced food. The guests would go away content, their bellies warm with tasty food. 'Shobha's vessels have barkat,' they said.

My father had constructed our house next to my maternal uncle's at Ma's insistence. Their family had fled Baramulla in north Kashmir during the tribal invasion of 1947. As a toddler, Ma had been carried by her 10-year-old brother on his back for miles to safety.

In constructing the house, my father had exhausted his entire Provident Fund; whatever little jewellery my mother possessed was also sold to help finance the construction. My father often talked about how he started the first phase of construction when he had only 3,600 rupees in his pocket. The other part of the house was built by two of my father's brothers. So in one house, we had three homes. The house was built in one of the new suburbs of Srinagar.

I was born a year after my parents moved to the new house. There were very few houses in our neighbourhood at that time, and ours didn't even have a boundary wall. Shepherds brought their flocks to graze in the open space around our house. The only theft that ever occurred was when a thief stole a bulb and a pair of old rubber slippers that belonged to my father from our veranda. There was a pair of new rubber slippers there as well, but the thief was considerate enough to leave them behind. As I was growing up, the house was also built up bit by bit. A boundary wall came up and pillars were built in the veranda. Smooth red cement was laid in the corridor and wardrobes and cupboards were built in the rooms. We also owned a black and white Weston television that took several minutes to warm up before coming to life. In those days, all of us would be excited about the feature film telecast on Doordarshan on Sunday evenings. Gradually, other families occupied the locality as well.

After escaping from Baramulla in 1947, most of my mother's family had relocated to Habba Kadal, an old locality in Srinagar named after the sixteenth-century Kashmiri poetess Habba Khatoon, who wrote beautiful verses of love and longing. My father's family came from a village in central Kashmir. My father's father was a Sanskrit scholar and he also dabbled in astrology to make ends meet. He had borne extreme hardships to raise his family. During a period of severe food scarcity in the 1950s, he had saved a sack of rice from a gang of robbers by jumping into a ditch overgrown with nettle grass. For days after, mudpacks had to be applied to his body to provide him relief. Every morning, even in the harshest winter, he would wake up in the ambrosial hours and walk to the shrine of our family goddess and recite the *Durgasaptashati*.

Everything in my grandfather's house was done with extreme care, as per Hindu tradition. Early in the morning, grandmother would clean her kitchen, applying a paste of mud and dried straw over its walls for purification. No onions or garlic were allowed. Often, my grandfather would invite home the sadhus and ascetics and scholars who came to the Kshir Bhawani shrine from all over India. Some were believed to have supreme yogic powers—one of them, it was said, could pull out his intestines from his mouth, wash them and push them back in. Grandfather was particularly fond of an ascetic from Bengal who visited the Valley in the summer. He would sit on a straw mat, speak very little, and would only drink a glass of sugarless milk. I have faint memories of him talking to me. One summer he did not return and we never saw him again.

Grandmother was betrothed to Grandfather at the age of thirteen. She would remember those days with a faint smile on her lips, of how difficult it was to cope with her father-in-law, who was a widower and prone to opium-induced aggression, and would come home late in the night and demand a curry of dried fish spicy enough to set the rice afire.

In Father's village, many things could be obtained through the barter system. The family grew paddy and kept some cows as well. Often, fishermen, plying their shikaras along the small river that flowed past the house, would give fish in exchange for rice. Food was easy to come by in villages. But in the city, it was harder. After finishing school, Father had to stay with his aunt in Srinagar to attend college. It was difficult to feed an extra person. Often, my father said, he would buy a sesame bagel from the baker, moisten it with water and eat it for lunch.

In those days the results of the Board Exams would be declared on the radio. The day Father's higher secondary exam results were to be declared, he sat glued to it. But they wouldn't announce his name. Distraught, he thought he had failed. But it turned out to be a mistake. Afterwards, at his father's insistence, my father joined government service and worked with the irrigation department.

It was in the city that my parents met and later got married. Around that time, there was tension in the Valley. Riots had broken out over an episode of a Pandit girl marrying a Muslim boy. The Pandits had risen in a rare gesture and launched an agitation. On the day my parents got married, curfew had been declared in some parts of the Valley.

After the wedding ceremony, the newly-wed couple arrived at my father's village in a tonga. It had rained earlier, and there was muddy slush all around, and heaps of dried straw had to be put on the road to enable the bride from the city to walk without getting her shoes soiled. For years my mother would taunt Father about that particular evening.

Ma was hard-working. She would often carry dirty utensils in sub-zero temperatures to wash them under a tap in a corner of the street in Habba Kadal where she lived with her parents before marriage. She was also known to have climbed up on the tin roof of their house wearing her brother's Duckback gumboots to shovel down the snow lest the roof collapsed under its weight—a feat that only the most courageous men could achieve. It was this spirit that led her to start working right after completing her education, choosing not to be a housewife. She served in the state health department.

One of my earliest memories is of her wearing a red sweater with a floral pattern. It was much later that I came to know it was a gift from my father, who had ordered it from Amritsar through a visiting cousin. For years, I think, the image of India for an ordinary Kashmiri was restricted to Punjab—to Amritsar and Ludhiana. Kashmiris went to Delhi, or Bombay, or Calcutta, but any non-Kashmiri was a Punjabi for them.

For many years after their marriage, my parents served in far-flung villages where people were so innocent that some of them believed that the Hindu nationalist party, the Jan Sangh, was a demon that pounced upon hapless people were they to be found alone in the fields. Sometimes Father and Ma would come to the city and watch movies at the Palladium cinema—old films with soulful Mukesh and Rafi songs. One of my mother's favourites was a song from *Awaara*, where Nargis wished that the moon would turn its face away from them for a moment so that she could love Raj Kapoor. I often found her humming this song to herself at home.

I was born at a time when double-decker buses had just been introduced on certain routes and I vaguely remember that a ride from Lal Chowk to our locality would cost twenty-five paisa.

My sister had been born six years earlier. The clock tower in the main square in Srinagar intrigued me since it looked so ancient and never kept the correct time. It stood like an old patriarch in the middle of the city. It was next to this clock tower that Jawaharlal Nehru had climbed atop a table, along with Sheikh Mohammed Abdullah, and had spoken about India's commitment to Kashmir and its people.

In the early eighties, I remember visits to the ancient Shankaracharya temple built on a hill overlooking Srinagar city. The temple was named after the Hindu philosopher-saint Adi Shankaracharya, who is believed to have visited the temple in the ninth century. We also visited the shrine of Kashmir's patron goddess Sharika inside the Hari Parbat Fort. On Basant Panchami, we would go for day-long excursions to the Ramchandra temple in Srinagar.

My mother's sister lived near the cantonment area, and my uncle was a movie buff. Hoping to catch a glimpse of some film stars, my uncle would seat me on the crossbar of his bicycle and ride to the Oberoi hotel, where most film stars stayed. He was so fond of movies that he would often sit all night long in front of the television, keeping the volume low, smoking Panama cigarettes and noting down the cast with a pencil on a wall next to him. I was amazed by his skill in recognizing old film actresses: Nimmi, Suraiya, Geeta Bali, Bina Rai, Nalini Jaywant. It was the time when the actress Tabassum would appear on television with a rose in her hair, hosting a film-based programme. I also remember watching the singer Hemant Kumar on her show, a shawl placed neatly on his left shoulder, his head tilted towards the right as he sang one soulful song after another. Besides these outings and the Sunday evening feature film on television, the only source of entertainment was listening to stories from our grandparents. And then there were family gatherings and festivals.

Being Shaivites—followers of Lord Shiva—the most important among our festivals was Shivratri, which would be celebrated over a period of one week or so. It falls in either February or March, during the severe cold. Preparations would begin a month earlier. The whole house would be thoroughly cleaned and the larder replenished. Two days before the festival, Father and I would visit Habba Kadal to buy pooja paraphernalia from Kanth Joo, a toothless man who ran a small shop as ancient and mysterious as its owner. From there, we would go to the Muslim potter who sold us earthen pots, and the Shivling for rituals. Then we would make our way to the bridge—one of the eight built across the Jhelum—and bargain with the fishermen for the best rates.

We would return home, Father and I, while I held his hand and a bag of roasted chestnuts. At home, Father would clean the fish in a basin and scrape off the scales under a tap beside the kitchen garden, while I watched in fascination as he cut open its guts and sliced the fish into pieces. We children would wait for the fish bladders to be extricated so that we could jump on them, making them produce a noise while bursting. I would then help Father make garlands and little round thrones for Shiva and his bride Parvati from dried straw.

On the evening of the festival, an area in the kitchen would be cleared to conduct the 'marriage rituals'. The seat of prominence would be given to Parvati, represented by an earthen pitcher. It would be filled with water, and the choicest walnuts and sugar cones. Its neck would be decorated with marigold and bhelpatra strings, vermillion mixed with clarified butter, and silver foil. The rituals lasted till midnight. As children we would struggle to remain awake till the 'marriage' was solemnized. The next day, scores of lamb, fish and vegetable dishes would be prepared, and the elders would give money to the children to buy anything we wanted. During the day, the men gambled at cards while the children played *juph-taakh*, a game played with cowries. They symbolized fertility and playing with them was an old practice because of the dwindling population due to religious persecution and high infant mortality rates. The cowries were procured from Bombay by a Pandit family that had settled hundreds of years ago in Bajalta near Jammu. From there, the shells would be transported to the Valley on mules.

On the final evening of the festival, the 'bride' and the 'groom' would be bid farewell. Taken to the river, they would be immersed in its waters. Upon returning, the custom was for the farewell party to knock on the main door of the house. A family member would enquire who was at the door, and one of the members of the farewell party would respond, 'I've brought with me money, food, prosperity, and happiness.' It was then that the door would be opened and the farewell party welcomed back. Then walnuts from the pitcher, sweetened with milk and sugar, would be eaten along with rotis made of rice flour cooked on a slow fire.

Sometimes it snowed during Shivratri, and we would make snowmen in our garden. We had an unwavering belief in our gods and in our festivals. During Afghan rule in Kashmir, the Governor, Jabbar Khan, upon hearing that it invariably snowed on Shivratri, ordered that it be celebrated in June–July. But even on that night, due to some unusual atmospheric cooling, snowflakes fell, silencing the vicious.

∾

Vidyam deehe Saraswati . . . O Goddess of Learning, grant me knowledge. Under the apple tree that stood in our garden, like a sage doing penance, Grandfather made me recite this hymn after him. He told me how, when I was an infant, he had dipped a wooden nib in honey and written on my tongue one syllable that would guide my life: Om. It was the key to all secrets, he said, that I ever wished to have unravelled. It was an antidote to all poisons that would try to ride on my breath. It would keep rabid dogs away from me and, likewise, *Rahchok*, the Will-o'-the-wisp—the one with a bowl of fire placed on his head who misled people towards doom when the earth was covered with snow. Its recital would bar bad thoughts from polluting my mind; it would keep me from harm's way, no matter what shape or form it took.

One room in our house was dedicated to the pursuit of knowledge. Its wooden shelves were lined with books, some of them covered with brown paper. *The Complete Works of Swami Vivekananda. Arabian Nights.* Kalhana's *Rajatarangini.* Gandhi's *The Story of My Experiments with Truth.* Tagore's *Gitanjali.* Phanishwar Nath Renu's *Jaloos.* The collected stories of Premchand and Saadat Hasan Manto. These would be brought out on a particular day in spring, and worshipped. The night before, Ma would fill a brass plate with grains of rice over which she placed a pen, a portrait of the goddess, some milk in a small bowl, and a bunch of narcissus flowers. The next morning we were required to first look at this offering—that was how we welcomed the coming of the new year, praying that we acquired a few more droplets from the ocean of knowledge. *Vidyam deehe Saraswati.*

Apart from these old customs, there was a thumb rule that guided our lives. You could say it was a story the moral of which was left unsaid, deliberately, I think. It was too evident, too stark for even a dimwit to miss. The story went like this: Two boys got into a verbal duel in downtown Srinagar. It turned into a fistfight and, in no time, the two lay on the road, with one boy overpowering the other. As he lay over him, the stronger boy's sacred thread which identified him as a Pandit, became visible.

'Bloody hell, you are a Pandit!' shouted one boy. In a moment, the tables turned and it was the other boy who won the fight. The fact that his opponent was a Pandit gave the other boy strength. Nobody was expected to lose to a Kashmiri Pandit in a physical fight.

No one knew exactly when this apocryphal fight had occurred. I had heard this story many times from men who belonged to my grandfather's generation and from those of my father's generation as well. It had probably trickled down, this piece of wisdom, from generation to generation.

I didn't read much into the story as a child, but I remember creating quite a scene after hearing my parents discuss my thread-wearing ceremony.

'Why, son?' my grandfather pulled me onto his lap. 'All of us have done it. My father, me, your father, and now you. This is what distinguishes us, and makes us who we are: Brahmins,' he tried to reason it out with me. My groans grew louder and I flailed my arms.

'All right, tell me why you don't want us to put the *janeu* around your shoulder?' he finally asked.

I remained silent for a while. And then I said it.

'Because, then Tariq will know that I'm a Pandit and he will overpower me.'

I don't quite remember how Grandfather reacted to what I said. Perhaps he laughed as he always did at my childish remarks.

Tariq was my friend in school. A photo of the class of 1984 I once possessed showed him next to me, his arm over my shoulder. It was the same year that the school magazine had a portrait of the goddess Saraswati on its front page.

On the afternoon of the day the magazine was distributed among the students, some of us were playing cricket on the school grounds. In the classroom, Tariq and I were inseparable, thick as thieves, as our English teacher said. But on the playground we were arch-enemies—he was Javed Miandad, the famous Pakistani batsman, while I was Kapil Dev, the great Indian fast bowler. With a tennis ball and a bat made of a broken wooden plank, we would put up the fight of our lives. Most days, Tariq's side won, but that day it was my turn. On the last ball, bowled by Tariq himself, I hit a sixer. My team won the match.

Later, on my way back to the classroom, I saw a group of my classmates standing in a circle.

'India won the match,' I shouted. They would be crestfallen, I knew, since all of them supported Tariq's team, which called itself 'Pakistan'. They would all hurl abuses when the national anthem was sung during the school assembly and kicked those of us who sang it. One of them looked at me, and then all of them ran away suddenly, throwing a bunch of papers on to the floor. I thought my victory had embarrassed them. But what were the papers they had left behind? I picked one up, and recoiled in disgust—the paper was covered with snot. I threw it away. It was then that my eyes fell on another, partially crumpled paper. A shiver ran through my body. It was a page torn from the school magazine—it was the portrait of the goddess Saraswati. It was covered with snot too. My heart sank and my stomach felt as if someone had punched me. I was very scared. I thought the goddess would punish me for my friends' behaviour. *Vidyam deehe Saraswati*. No more. I raced out towards the grounds to report the incident to Tariq.

I ran through one corridor and entered another. At one end in semi-darkness, I saw Tariq, his head bent over something. I slowed down. He didn't notice me. It was then that he tore off something from what lay on his lap and brought it towards his face.

'Tariq!' I called out.

He was startled. The page fell from his hands. He got up and just ran away. I prayed that it wouldn't be what I thought it was. I was paralysed, unable to move. After what must have been a minute, I finally walked towards the page. I didn't have to pick it up. The goddess's musical instrument—the Veena—was clearly visible. I kept staring at it, transfixed. It was when the school bell rang that my trance broke. I lifted the page, carefully folded it, and put it in the pocket of my shorts.

I didn't tell anyone about this incident. Tariq avoided me for many days. Afterwards, when he spoke to me, I tried to avoid thinking of that day. He never mentioned it either. We got back to our respective roles in the playground.

But I don't remember us putting our arms around each other ever again.

Sometimes, glimpses of Kashmir are shown on the Discovery Channel. One day Father spotted the Dal Lake, and he almost shouted, pointing it out to my niece: 'Look, this is where *nadru* comes from!' He had forgotten that the lotus stem we sometimes bought in Delhi might have been grown in the polluted Yamuna waters, for all we knew. But I didn't say anything.

My parents shifted to Delhi from Jammu in 1998, a year after getting my sister married. Three weeks before they shifted, Ma paid me her first visit in Delhi. I went to receive her at the interstate bus terminus; she refused to travel by train, which she found filthy. In the autorickshaw, on our ride home, she had a good look at me and her eyes moistened. I was working for a television news channel at that time and kept long hours, often skipping meals. I had lost weight and this made her unhappy.

'You have grown so thin,' she said.

'Girls here like slim boys,' I quipped.

But Ma was not one to appreciate humour. 'I hope some Punjabi girl has not cast her spell on you,' she said with genuine worry.

She spent three days in Delhi, and I took her around to show her the sights. I also bought her kulfi, which she relished. I knew that, unlike my father, for whom a proper meal had to include rice, Ma relished hot, crispy tandoori rotis. So we ate at a small, clean restaurant where she had two rotis with a bowl of dal and cauliflower.

One Monday morning, three weeks after Ma's visit—Monday was my day off and they knew it—my parents landed up at the doorstep of my one-room flat. I was surprised to see them and shocked to see the number of items they had brought along with them. I was not even sure so many things would fit into my room. But in two hours, Ma had set up a kitchen. From the Kashmir Valley, we had been forced to shift to Jammu. And now, from Jammu, my parents had come to Delhi.

The day after, when I returned from work close to midnight, I saw Father pacing in the balcony. There were no cell phones then, and he didn't have my office numbers. 'That is why I had been dissuading you from shifting here,' I said before he could complain. Father remained silent.

'Eat your food,' Ma said. She had cooked some of my favourite Kashmiri delicacies.

It took my parents months to come to terms with my gruelling work schedule. Sometimes, when I returned home visibly tired, Ma would ask: 'So, how much do you earn?' After I told her, she would say, 'Sit at home, I'll give you a thousand more than that!' Gradually, they became used to it. So much so that if I got home early, they would ask if all was well.

Wherever we went, moving from one flat to another, Father forged friendships with vegetable vendors, owners of daily utility stores, and with electricians and plumbers. Wherever we lived, few knew me by my name. They only referred to me as Pandita sahab's son.

Every few months my parents would go to Jammu to catch up with relatives who had settled there after the exodus of 1990. After Ma permanently took to her bed, in 2004, they were unable to return. So, our only contact with the family is on the phone or when relatives come to Delhi for short visits. When they come from Jammu, my relatives bring with them souvenirs from home: collard greens, raw walnuts, or sesame bagels made by Kashmiri bakers who have now set up shop in Jammu. Sometimes Father forgets that he is not even in Jammu now, that he is even further away from home. So he sometimes refers to Jammu as 'Shahar', or city—Shahar was always meant to refer to Srinagar. That is a habit my father's generation has: calling Srinagar 'Shahar'—the city that is home. And when I gently remind Father of his mistake, he smiles an embarrassed smile. But for days afterwards, he goes silent. For days, he does not read the newspapers. For days, he does not watch Doordarshan Kashmir and hum along with Rashid Hafiz. I can only imagine what images the mere mention of Shahar evokes in him.

Shahar was our home. Shahar was our *shahrag*—our jugular. Shahar was us.

In Shahar though, by the age children learned the alphabet, they realized that there was an irreversible bitterness between Kashmir and India, and that the minority Pandits were often at the receiving end of the wrath this bitterness evoked. We were the punching bags. But we assimilated noiselessly, and whenever one of us became a victim of selective targetting, the rest of us would lie low, hoping for things to normalize.

But Shahar was also about friendships, bonding, compassion, and what the elders called 'lihaaz', which, in simple terms, means consideration. But in the Kashmiri context, it was many things. It was throwing away a cigarette if one spotted an elder approaching. It was offering a seat in the bus to a woman from one's locality. It was taking a heavy bag from an old man's hand and carrying it till his house.

Sometimes during a summer sunset, when the sky turned crimson, serene old men taking leisurely puffs from their hookahs would look at it and then sigh and say, 'There has been *khoonrizi*—bloodshed—somewhere.'

On Eid-ul-Zuha, we would go to our neighbours' homes to wish them happiness. One of my father's Muslim friends lived nearby, and when Father would be out on long official tours, he would stop by, knocking gently at our door, refusing to come inside, and asking if we needed anything. My sister sometimes taught his children, and on Eid-ul-Zuha I would slip out and visit his house to watch their family sacrifice sheep. A piece of lamb's meat would later be sent to us, uncooked, because some families avoided eating at each other's house for religious considerations. Though, by the time of my father's generation, these considerations had almost been dissolved. Our neighbours wished us on Shivratri, and we would offer them walnuts soaked in sweet milk and water.

We hardly knew of life beyond Kashmir. I remember a cousin had gone to Meerut to study agricultural science. On returning, he would tell us how common murders were there, and I remember how a hush fell when he recounted how a man had been called out of his home late in the night and then stabbed. In the Valley, the biggest crime we had heard about was how in a fight sometimes a man would pull out his kangri from underneath his pheran and hurl it at his opponent. When somebody fought or used foul language, he would be immediately dubbed a *'Haaen'z'*—a member of the boatman community, known for their crude language and whose wives apparently fought bitterly.

But this lihaaz, this peaceful coexistence, would be threatened every now and then. It was as if the minority Pandits were to be blamed for everything that went wrong. It could be anything, as our experience would tell us.

In 1986, major anti-Pandit riots broke out in Anantnag in southern Kashmir in retaliation to rumours that Muslims had been killed in the Hindu-majority region of Jammu. Some believed the riots were a conspiracy by one political party to bring down another party's government. Whatever the reasons, the Pandits became the target. Houses were looted and burnt down, men beaten up, women raped and dozens of temples destroyed. A massive statue of the goddess Durga was brought down in the ancient Lok Bhawan temple.

A few years earlier, in our locality, a few Pandit families had tried to construct a small temple out of wooden planks. Although there was a temple nearby, during the harsh winters the snow would make it difficult to walk on the road, so some families thought of building a temple closer to their homes. But as soon as the planks were assembled and the idols placed on a small, wooden platform, some Muslim men gathered and began to hurl abuses. One of them brought the whole structure down with a kick. There was no protest. We had learnt to live that way. Whenever things went sour, we would just lower our heads and walk away. Or stay at home, till things got better. I remember visiting the site a few hours later when some of the Pandit families were carrying away their desecrated gods. I was heartbroken at the sight of a broken idol of Hanuman. For us children, he was like Superman. We would sing his praises in the form of the *Hanuman Chalisa*.

I returned home and hid myself in a patch of our garden, and lay there, face down. I must have stayed like that for a few hours till Totha came looking for me. Totha was Tathya's younger brother, and he lived alone in a small room in his brother's house.

Totha turned me over onto my back and I held him tight. 'They broke the temple,' I said. He was silent for a while. And then he spoke. 'You know, Swami Vivekananda—his photo is in our *thokur kuth*—he came to the Kshir Bhawani temple many years ago and spent a few days alone there. While performing a yagna, he had a vision of the goddess. "Mother," he addressed her, "I am so disturbed; everywhere I see temples being destroyed by Muslim invaders." That is when the goddess spoke to him. "It doesn't matter if they enter my temple and desecrate my idol. It should not matter to you. Tell me, do you protect me, or do I protect you?"'

Totha then held my hand and led me to his small room. From the pocket of his Nehru jacket, he pulled out a stick. 'I got this for you,' he said.

'What, you got me a stick!' I cried.

He smiled. 'Bite into it.'

I did as instructed and was overjoyed. I had never tasted sugar cane before. Totha was like that—full of surprises. God knows where he had got that sugar cane from, since it was not grown in the Valley.

The dose of sugar calmed me down, and I soon forgot about the incident. But I think it changed me a little, and I became conscious of my identity as a Kashmiri Pandit. A few weeks later, my paternal grandfather came to visit us for a few days. He was quite old now and spent most of his time in prayer. Even when we children created bedlam while playing around him, he would not even raise an eyebrow. One day I stopped playing and sat next to him while he recited his prayers. I waited patiently, and as soon as he finished and opened his eyes, I asked him what prayer he was reciting.

'*Durgasaptashati*,' he replied.

'Is it the same one that is supposed to have so much energy that some people lose their mental balance while reciting it?'

'Yes, that is the one.'

'So how come you can recite it and nothing happens to you?'

He laughed and said, 'I don't know, son. Maybe one has to prepare oneself for it. It has taken me years to ready myself.'

'So teach me how to recite it, won't you?'

'No, son, you are young right now. It requires a lot of patience, a lot of discipline. You don't even bathe everyday. When you grow up, I'll teach you.'

I threw a tantrum. I insisted that until my grandfather taught me how to recite the mantra, I wouldn't eat. Nobody took me seriously at first. But when I did not eat the whole day, Father got angry and stormed into my room.

'Don't be a fool; come and eat.'

I was quite afraid of him, but that day I held my ground. In the evening, Ma said Grandfather wanted to see me.

'Okay, I will teach you a portion of it,' he said. And he did. I practised it for days and learnt it by heart.

My faith in what Grandfather taught me that day has never wavered. I've tested that mantra in the most adverse moments of my life. And it has never failed me.

Totha lived in a small room on the first floor, overlooking the kitchen garden. Though he lived with his brother's family, he was fairly independent. He washed his own clothes and refused to use modern detergents, using instead a crude soap he got from the Khatri shopkeepers in Maharaj Ganj. He ate frugally and was not fussy about what he ate. He was a chain smoker, and in the evening he would come to our house and Ma would give him tea in a steel tumbler. He never used a cushion and always sat erect with his right leg resting on his left. I think in the evenings he felt a little lonely. My uncle worked as a teacher and was posted in distant villages for long periods, and my aunt would be busy in the kitchen. Whatever spare time she had, she liked to spend with her friends in the neighbourhood. The two children went to college and had no time to spare either. So Totha came to us in the evenings and told stories about his postings in Ladakh and Gilgit to my father who always listened patiently to him. He had served in these places before Independence. Later he worked in the Chest Disease hospital in Srinagar. Totha had diabetes and one day I asked him what that meant.

'That means there is sugar in my urine,' he said.

I had seen him pissing sometimes beside a shrub behind their house. After he said that, I went several times to that spot, hoping to find grains of sugar.

Totha used to pamper us. Every day he brought us something new—an Ajanta fountain pen, a toy pistol, a packet of lotus seeds, a roll of Poppins candy, Amul milk chocolate, digestive pills, elaichi-flavoured toffees.

Behind our house was stationed a battalion of the Border Security Force (BSF), and sometimes we crossed the barbed wire and sneaked in to steal shuttlecocks after the officers had played their game of badminton. In the mornings and evenings, the soldiers sounded the bugle and we children would imitate its sound.

Sometimes, Mother would take us to a wedding feast. A huge tent would be erected, and inside, long strips of white cloth laid on the ground and guests seated on either side of them. Two boys would come bearing a basin of water, a cake of soap, and a towel for the guests to wipe their hands with. Then, one by one, men who were relatives or friends or neighbours of the bride or groom, would come with brass plates, and then dishes of food and rice. The quantity of food put on one's plate depended on one's age, with the elders receiving the most generous helpings. The head cook would come out last, doling out portions of the main dish. If there was an important guest—like a son-in-law—he would be accorded special treatment, which often meant someone from his wife's family would hover around him, instructing the men who carried the meat dishes to put additional helpings on his plate.

At our marriages, Muslim women celebrated with us by linking their arms and singing traditional songs to welcome the

groom and his family and friends. My mother's best friend was
Shahzaad. She also worked with the health department. They
travelled together to distant villages for work, and shopped
together, and exchanged gossip, and bitched about their mothers-
in-law.

Kashmiris have a way with nicknames. In old Srinagar, there
lived a man called Jawahar Lal who was a fan of Sartre and
would always be seen carrying one of his books. His neighbours
named him 'Javv'e Sartre'. In Habba Kadal, there lived an
eccentric professor who had been named 'Deen'e Phil'asafer'
(the professor's name, I believe, was Dina Nath). The locals
said he was often to be seen on the bridge mumbling
mathematical equations to himself. One of them supposedly
went like this: 'I'm on bridge, bridge is on water, bridge-bridge
cancel, I'm on water.'

My parents were protective, and I think their lives revolved
around their home and the welfare of their children. There are
sepia pictures of my parents enjoying day-long picnics at the
Mughal Gardens. In some of them, my father sports a Dev
Anand puff while Ma wears a sari like the dazzling Waheeda
Rehman. But after we were born, their entire focus shifted to
our education and well-being. Whatever money was saved was
spent on the house. Ma ran the affairs of the house like a
seasoned manager. She knew exactly what was kept where—
dried chillies, woollen socks, coal powder, candles.

After office, many men would typically go to a bar to have a
drink discreetly and then savour lamb mince kebabs at roadside
stalls in Lal Chowk. These were made by Muslims, and some
Pandits found it a little embarrassing to be spotted in front of
these stalls. So, they would place their order quickly and then
stand in a corner, as if waiting for something else. Once the

kebabs were made, the man signalled, and the Pandit would come and quickly gobble them up.

But Father returned home at six on the dot, ringing the fish-shaped bell that I had chosen, and my sister and I would rush to receive him at the door. He would come inside, change, and drink his tea and talk to Ma.

I remember once Ma and her entire family had gone to Baramulla for a cousin's wedding. My sister and I stayed back with Father. In the afternoon, he got us dressed and said that we were going to watch a movie. We took an autorickshaw to the Broadway cinema where they were showing *Hero*. Back in school, some classmates had already seen it and had begun to sport red headbands as Jackie Shroff had done in the film.

We reached the cinema hall well in time, but the queue for tickets had spilled out on to the main road and by the look of it we knew that we had no chance.

'Wait, I'll go to Moti Lal, he will surely manage,' Father said. Moti Lal lived on our street and was the manager of the cinema. Father got us a softie cone each and asked us to wait for him. After a while he returned, empty-handed.

'Did you get the tickets?' I asked him. He said nothing. After a minute he told us that Moti Lal had seen him but had turned his head away. Father understood that he was avoiding him. He must have realized that my Father might ask him for help with tickets. So Father returned without talking to him.

'Are we to go back without watching the film?' I asked.

'Oh no, never,' he said. 'Have faith.'

We waited and after a while a shady-looking man passed by. Father went after him, and from a distance we saw him speaking to the man. I almost shouted when I saw him handing over the pink slips that I knew were tickets to my father. He had bought the tickets in black. He held our hands and in no time we were inside the hall with popcorn and Gold Spot, watching Jackie Shroff with his red headgear, performing stunts on his motorbike.

That day my father became my hero.

In early 1984, one name came up repeatedly during after-dinner conversations between my father and my two uncles—Bhindranwale. From what I gathered, he was some kind of Sikh leader and had taken control of the Golden Temple in Amritsar. My mother often raved about the Golden Temple; it was the only place she had visited outside Kashmir. She had very fond memories of visiting it and more than anything else, she had been impressed with the cleanliness of the entire complex.

It was a hot day in June 1984 when the news began to trickle in that something dangerous was happening in Amritsar. The Indian army, we learnt, had attacked the temple to get rid of Bhindranwale. Mother was sad to see the desecration. She kept describing how the temple looked from inside and how peaceful one felt there while the Sikh priests sang the soulful gurbani. That evening, one of father's friends came by and told us that in retaliation to the army operation, a mob had descended upon the Hanuman temple in Amira Kadal and thrown the idol into the Jhelum. The priests were beaten up as well. I couldn't understand why the Hanuman temple had been targeted for what had transpired hundreds of miles away, events in which Kashmir had no role to play.

It was in October of the same year that Indira Gandhi, who many held responsible for the assault on the Golden Temple, was assassinated by her Sikh bodyguards. I had skipped school that day for some reason and in the afternoon we heard the news on All India Radio that the prime minister had been shot, and that she was in critical condition. It was later in the day that the BBC finally declared her dead.

The radio had begun to play the mournful shehnai. My sister returned from school in tears that day. She said there had been celebrations in her school and on the streets. The previous year Mrs Gandhi had visited Kashmir and she had addressed a rally in Iqbal Park where men sat in the front row naked, waving their genitals at her. It is not that we were traditional Congress supporters, or for that matter followers of politics. I don't remember anyone in my family stepping out on election days. They had neither the time nor the inclination for it. But for us, Indira Gandhi represented the emotional connect we felt with India, or more specifically with Jawaharlal Nehru, who we thought of as one of our own.

In Delhi, the anti-Sikh riots began soon after Mrs Gandhi was declared dead. From the *Indian Express*, we learnt the horrific details of how scores of innocent people were done to death for no fault of theirs. 'One day, something similar will happen here, to us,' one of my uncles said.

Five days after Mrs Gandhi's death, Dedda passed away too, in her sleep. She had begun to hallucinate about a person who she said was aiming at her with a gun from atop a tree in the backyard. Dedda's death came as a big blow to Totha. Tathya had died years ago, and so Dedda, his sister-in-law, had been Totha's only companion.

A year later, my paternal grandfather passed away as well. Ma had been visiting him in the hospital, and that night she asked father not to lay any elaborate bedding at home. She had a premonition of Grandfather's death. At midnight, we were woken up. Grandfather's body was brought home in an ambulance. The children of the house were made to put water into Grandfather's mouth with a spoon, and then we were sent to Totha's house for the night.

The following morning, Grandfather was taken on his final journey. As my father and uncles lifted up his bier, I silently recited the prayer he had taught me not very long ago.

I don't know what Shahar means to me personally. In so many ways, we were protected in Shahar from the trickery and the treachery of big cities like Delhi. In Shahar, as I realized later, speaking one's own language meant so much. It filled one with contentment and an undefinable happiness. From the late 1990s onwards, years after the exodus, when I went to the Valley on reporting assignments, it was as if a tap opened up suddenly. Kashmiri words did a foxtrot on my tongue and I uttered them—words that I had forgotten even existed. Once, in the dead of the night, when nobody was out on the streets except army convoys, I sneaked out from my hotel with a few local friends and sat on a wooden deck that extended out over the Dal Lake. A radio crackled somewhere in one of the houseboats, and the Hazratbal shrine shimmered in the still waters of the lake. A lone light, perhaps from a sentry post, shone from the Hari Parbat Fort. We sat there, taking swigs from a bottle of Old Monk rum, and laughed over a tragicomic incident a friend was narrating—

A few years ago, early one morning, hundreds of army troopers surrounded a village. They said they were looking for militants.

This was in the early 2000s, and by then the Kashmiris were quite used to the humiliation of being made to assemble in a ground while soldiers conducted searches inside houses. Such search operations—the Kashmiris called them 'crackdowns'—would sometimes last for the entire day.

In this village the men were made to assemble in a school ground. They sat on their haunches while soldiers, wearing bulletproof jackets and helmets, kept a watch on them. A man had the urge to shit, and it made him restless. He looked at the soldier hovering over him, held his chin (that is how Kashmiris ask for a favour) and muttered: *Sahab, gussa aa raha hai.*

Now, in Kashmiri, *guss* means shit, and in Hindi, *gussa* means anger. The man thought by adding an 'a', a Kashmiri word could turn into a Hindi one. It did, but unfortunately it meant something else now. The soldier let out an expletive and almost hit the man on his head. 'Bastard,' he shouted, 'we have not been here for five minutes and you are already feeling angry!'

It was then that the man's neighbour pitched in to explain his friend's predicament. 'Sahab,' he begged, 'he doesn't know Hindi. He means: *Usko gobar aaya hai.*' *Gobar* in Hindi means dung. He must have remembered some school essay on the cow. The soldier's rifle slipped off as he collapsed on the ground with uncontrollable laughter.

While we laughed as well, the story also filled my heart with sadness. And I was sure it saddened my friends as well. They had to live through this every day. But we did not share sadness beyond this. Because then the topic always veered towards the events of 1989–90, and that was the point at which our truths became different. For them, the events of 1990 were a rebellion against the Indian state. For me, these same events had led to exile and permanent homelessness. When I visited we laughed most times, and sang songs, and hugged each other.

Sometimes we just sat quietly, and at times like these, even the crackle of burning cigarette paper could be heard.

At times like these I remembered a girl.

When we were still in the Valley, at home, one of my distant cousins ended her life by jumping into the Jhelum. At first she was thought to have gone missing, and there were rumours of her having eloped with her lover. Apparently, for weeks before she disappeared, she had sat in a corner of her house, listening to a Rashid Hafiz song:

> *Yeli chhe myonuy maqbar sajawakh, paanay pashtaavakh*
> *Asmaan'ik taarakh ganzraavakh, paanay pashtaavakh*

> You will repent only when you decorate my grave
> You will count stars in the sky, this is how you will repent

They found her bloated body a week or so later in the river waters somewhere far away. Since I was young, I was not allowed to attend her cremation. I had met her for the first time when Grandfather passed away and her family stayed with us through the days of rituals. I had played cricket with her younger brother, and spent hours looking at her in secret admiration of her nail paint, and of the lipstick she hid in the pocket of her pheran, and of her diary in which she had copied verses of Rumi.

Her death left some indelible mark in my heart, some sort of pain—as if she had jumped into the Jhelum to meet me, and I was not there to save her, to rescue her. She must have been very lonely, or in love, or both.

For years afterwards, whenever I thought of homelessness, or when I heard singers at marriage ceremonies, I always remembered her. I thought of the spot from where she must have met the waters of the Jhelum. I also remembered a moment when she winked at me from behind the staircase of my home, where she sat writing something in her diary, and how she then kissed me on my cheek.

Her memory always makes that dull throbbing pain return—the pain of being in exile.

During summers in the Valley, we would shift to the first floor of our house. I didn't quite understand the logic, but I believe it was to take advantage of the cool breeze that blew during the nights. In Kashmir, no ceiling fans or refrigerators were required. A table fan was good enough. You returned from outside and sat in front of the fan till it dried off your sweat. That was it. On hot summer nights, you kept the windows open and wrapped yourself in thin white bed sheets.

On one such night, I had a nightmare. It must have been 1987. I saw that the space between my uncle's house and ours—that was where our kitchen gardens were—was infested with sword-wielding marauders who wore sandals made of dry straw. That was how Grandfather had described the tribal invaders who entered Kashmir in 1947. In my nightmare, the marauders went on a killing spree, thrusting their bayonets and swords into people. We were scared, and we tried to hide behind a wardrobe. That was when a few marauders caught hold of Ravi. One of them plunged his sword into Ravi's abdomen and he shouted for my mother. I woke up covered with beads of sweat. It was morning already, and everyone else had awoken. I was still dizzy with fear and couldn't get up. Then I heard the sound of a motorcycle and pulled myself to the window. I was happy to see Ravi alive and riding his motorcycle—perhaps to the university. I was so relieved that I shouted out to him. He didn't hear me and rode on.

Ravi was my maternal uncle's son. I was very fond of him and, more than me, my mother adored him. Among Kashmiris, the women have a strong attachment to their brother's children. But in my mother's case, it was much more than that.

Ravi was pursuing an MPhil in Botany. I never left him alone, and sometimes Ma had to drag me away from his room to give him some privacy. After all, he was a young man. For hours, he would be locked inside his room, a kangri under his pheran during the harsh winter months, listening to ghazals. When I was younger, I would get jealous of Jagjit Singh and Talat Aziz and maul their images on the audio cassettes with the long needle Ravi used to isolate anthers from flowers. He would look at their mauled faces and lift me in his arms, shadow boxing with me. He never complained. Sometimes he teased me by singing a ditty he had created using my nickname—

Vicky ko bhar do dickey mein, apna kaam karega.

Put Vicky in a dickey, he will do his work there.

I would watch him in fascination as he went about his routine. He would shave, filling water in a while enamelled cup, and I mentally made a note of the *Old Spice* aftershave he dabbed on his cheeks. Like him, I also stuck a poster of the cricketer Kris Srikkanth in my cupboard. Sometimes, he would give me gifts he acquired from his friends who worked in pharmaceutical companies—a plastic cat from Glaxo with an outdoor thermometer fitted in its guts, or a Brufen pocket paper-cutter. He had many friends, and he went out frequently with them. I would see them often sitting at a local provision store—the owner was their friend. But most times he would sit in his room, listening to his beloved ghazals and preparing notes and drawing botanical illustrations in his clear hand. For days, I remember, he tried to teach me how to correctly pronounce 'geography', and to irritate him, I would pronounce it incorrectly. It became a joke between us. When I think of those days, I reckon he must have been quite popular among girls of his age. Some of them would visit him every now and then, on the pretext of borrowing his notes or an audio cassette. He always wore jeans under his pheran. When I was a little older and found the traditional checked pyjamas we wore as children quite embarrassing, I understood why he did that.

Of all his friends, the kohl-eyed Latif Lone was closest to Ravi. The whole family knew him. We used to call him John Rambo. He was tall, muscular and always wore jeans and sneakers that he would top with a slim-fit pheran he had had specially stitched in the Bund area of Srinagar, famous for its tailors. Latif was a romantic and a big fan of Mohammed Rafi. He ran a small cosmetics shop called 'Bombay Beauties' and an electronics shop. The latter did not do much business, but he still ran it thinking it would fetch him an income someday. Also, it enabled him to listen to Rafi all the time, whose songs he would play amplified through a tall speaker.

I saw him often at Ravi's house, arguing about who the fastest bowler was in cricket. He also liked a cup of hot Lipton tea. In Kashmir, it was important to say what tea you wanted. Apart from the pink salt tea that most youngsters despised, there was the spiced kahwa. But it was considered 'hep' to sip on Lipton tea from bone china cups with flowery designs, just like the English did.

In those days, the state-run Doordarshan television network was quite boring, so in Kashmir we would extend our TV antennas as far as possible through the roof to catch the signals of Pakistan TV. I remember they had some really nice serials,

including a few for children. We particularly enjoyed *Alif Laila,*
based on the *Arabian Nights,* while the grownups wouldn't miss
a serial called *Emergency Ward.*

During the harsh winters it would snow heavily and in the
dead of the night we would wake up sometimes, startled by the
sound of a heavy load of snow falling from the tin roof, sounding
as if the sky were falling. Sometimes the snow also brought the
antenna down. Ravi would then be sent to fetch Latif Lone.
Latif would come, survey the antenna and then race up to the
attic from where he would climb atop the roof to fix the antenna
back into position. While clinging to the roof, he would invoke
the name of a Sufi saint: *Ya Peer Dasgeer.* The family would
meanwhile watch him from ground level, praying for his safety.
Sometimes Ravi's mother would curse herself for making him
do it.

Treth payen Pakistan Tv'eyus, she would lament. To hell with
Pakistan TV.

Latif would ask Ravi to straighten the antenna pole, look left
and then right, as if offering namaz, and finally fit the antenna.
'Now I want a cup of Lipton tea,' he would say. And so Latif
would have his tea while Ravi's mother and sister sat in front of
their TV to check how clear the signal had become.

I would sometimes spot Latif at Lal Chowk with a girl, and
sometimes they boarded the same bus as mine. And if I had a
seat and they didn't, I would offer mine to the girl. She would
smile and offer to seat me on her lap, but I always refused. I was
eleven then, almost a teenager. I wanted to stand, as Latif
did; and he would place his hand on my shoulder and it made
me proud.

Sometimes I visited his electronics shop to get songs recorded
on a cassette. I had no taste for Rafi then, and would want him

to record songs from films like *Dance Dance* and *Tridev*. Whenever I tried to pay him, he would take the money from my hand and put it back into my shirt pocket, whistling carelessly and breaking into some Rafi song. He sang them always.

In June 1983, as a seven-year-old, I have vague memories of the Indian cricket team's winning the World Cup. It was a day–night match; I fell asleep only to be woken later by shouts of celebration. But I remember everything of October 13, 1983. It was the day when the first ever international cricket match was played in Jammu and Kashmir. And the last, too. The Indian team and that of the West Indies arrived the day before the match and were put up in a hotel close to the Sher-e-Kashmir stadium. Ravi had somehow procured two tickets for the match, and we reached the stadium quite early, walking past sniffer dogs.

We took our seats on the freshly painted green benches. The two captains came down for the toss, which was won by the West Indies. They chose to field. I shouted in joy when a few minutes later Sunil Gavaskar and Kris Srikkanth entered the ground to open the batting for India.

And that was when it all began.

Ravi and I sat in disbelief as the stadium erupted with deafening cries of '*Pakistan zindabad!*' Green flags, both Pakistani and the identical Jamaat-e-Islami banner, were seen being carried by people in the stadium. Many in the crowd also held posters of Pakistani cricketers. The Indian batsmen looked like rabbits caught in glaring headlights. On the sixteenth ball he faced, Gavaskar was caught out, having scored only eleven runs. The whole team crumbled in 41 overs for a total score of 176 runs.

Later, as the West Indies team batted, the Indian fielders faced severe harassment. They were booed badly. A half-eaten apple was thrown at Dilip Vengsarkar, which hit him on his back.

Of course, India lost that match.

Years later, as a journalist, I met the cricketer Kirti Azad at a party. Azad was a part of the Indian team that day and had hit two defiant sixes in a lost cause. 'How can I ever forget that day?' he told me. 'It was like playing in Pakistan against Pakistan.'

Returning home after witnessing the madness, Ravi and I had not spoken a word. He tried to comfort me by treating me to a soft drink.

The next morning, I had avoided Rehman. But I also knew there would be no escaping him.

Rehman was our milkman. Every morning he came to our house, announcing his presence by shouting at the door. Most days, I would come out to collect the milk. We would argue with each other, about cricket and Pakistan. It used to be simple banter, but sometimes I would take it quite seriously.

'Where is he?' he asked my mother when she came out that morning to collect the milk. I was hiding behind the door.

'*Pakistan zindabad!*' he shouted, as if he felt my presence behind the door. My mother smiled.

'Tell your son that Gavaskar is a lamb in front of our Pakistani heroes,' he said.

I could no longer hold back. Though I was no fan of Gavaskar's, I felt I had to defend him. I stormed out to confront Rehman.

'All your Pakistani heroes are shit scared of Kris Srikkanth,' I said, on the verge of tears.

'There you are!' he said, and he laughed. 'The dal-eating Indians cannot fight Pakistan.'

'Are you a kid like him?' my mother intervened.

'This is war, *behnai*,' he said and looked mockingly at me.

'And you! You stop watching these matches,' my mother said. 'They mean nothing. It is just a game.'

But by then it was war indeed.

By 1986, forced blackouts were the norm in the Valley on India's Independence Day. In some places, if India won a cricket match against Pakistan, a stone could crash through one's windowpane and land in the bedroom. On April 18, 1986, India and Pakistan played against each other at Sharjah in the final of the Austral-Asia cup. In anticipation, I bullied Totha into buying me firecrackers from Maharaj Ganj.

On television, you could see Arab sheikhs in the VIP enclosure throw money in the air whenever a Pakistani batsman hit a boundary. But India managed to stay afloat.

The last over. My heart was pounding against my ribcage. The last ball. Pakistan needed four runs to win. Javed Miandad was on strike. Chetan Sharma was bowling. I had a matchbox in my hand. Sharma bowled a low full toss and Miandad hit it for a six. The stadium erupted. Miandad and number 11 batsman Tauseef Ahmed ran to the team pavilion, jubilant. My matchbox went limp with sweat. Every combustible item in the Sharjah ground was on fire.

A few minutes later, it was as if it were Diwali in Kashmir. I think every cracker available in Kashmir was burst in the next one hour. People streamed out of their houses and on to the streets chanting *Allah ho Akbar*. In the nippy April weather of the Valley, people drank gallons of Limca to celebrate, the way they had seen cricket stars celebrate with champagne.

And I lay huddled in a corner of my house.

Twenty-five years after that episode, in 2011, when we had been in exile for more than two decades, India registered a World Cup victory. I am grown up now, and victory or defeat in a cricket match means nothing to me. But my father had tears in his eyes when India won. He looked at me expectantly. I didn't have the heart to tell him that though I don't care any longer for cricket, my feelings from 1986 remain.

In *More Die of Heartbreak*, Saul Bellow calls such feelings 'first heart'. My first heart remains with that failed yorker bowled by Chetan Sharma.

During the summer vacations, I stayed at home while my parents were at work. Ma was always visiting some village or the other. When she returned in the evenings, her handbag would be full of small tokens of gratitude given by villagers who sought treatment at her health centre. Someone would fall from a walnut tree and get hurt badly. Or someone would accidentally be hurt with an axe or some other tool. Or a child would have a fever and Ma would provide the required medicine. Or an anaemic mother would get better because of a health supplement Ma recommended. Once they got well, the villagers would return and offer her apples, or raw walnuts, or almonds, or the juiciest of chestnuts, or a small packet of saffron. As children, we ransack her handbag and treated ourselves to its contents.

But sometimes, staying inside the house for the whole day would make me cranky. One day, out of sheer boredom, I asked Ravi if I could accompany him to the university. He sensed that I was down. 'Today, I have classes to attend. And anyway, there

is not much to show you at the university. But why don't you be
ready tomorrow morning and we will go for a small outing,' he
said. I was so excited that the moment Ma returned in the
evening, I told her about our plans.

I couldn't sleep for hours after Ma had tucked me into bed.
And when I finally did, I dreamt of the next day and the fun we
would have.

By sunrise the next morning I was wide awake. I put on my
best shirt and a pair of trousers father had bought for me from
the Blue Fox garment store and I waited for Ravi to wake up.

We set out in the early afternoon on his Yamaha bike. It was
a bright afternoon and in no time we left the hubbub of Lal
Chowk to enter the tranquil area of the Shankaracharya temple
near the foothills.

While riding on a long road, Ravi slowed down his bike and
asked me to look far ahead. 'Can you see water on the road?' he
asked. I looked intensely but couldn't see anything. Embarrassed,
I lied and said that I could.

'That is just an illusion. There is no water there, but in the
heat one imagines that there is. It is called a mirage,' Ravi explained.

'Oh yes, I see it clearly,' I lied again.

Our first stop was at the Shalimar Garden. We parked the
motorcycle next to photo studios where pictures of studio owners
with various film stars were displayed.

Inside the garden, Ravi bought a packet of red cherries and
we sat down under a tree like two old friends meeting after a
long time. He told me of an Austrian monk, Gregor Mendel,
who had devised the law of genetics using pea plants. He spoke
of other things as well, but by that time my attention was
diverted by a foreigner with green hair. She had perched herself
atop a tree, and below, her friend was beseeching her to climb

down. But she refused, and after every minute or so, would break into uncontrollable laughter. My school friends had told me how some foreigners consumed drugs. I had no idea what they meant and what drugs really were. I had heard of how foreigners carried 'brown sugar'. We thought sugar, if burnt in a pan, turned brown and acquired the properties of a drug. That day when I saw the green-haired woman, I thought she must have consumed brown sugar.

We thought of foreigners as either very educated and cultured—'Englishman type'—or bohemian. We loosely termed the latter as 'hippies' and even had a ditty for them:

Janana yeh ajab haal dekho, hippiyon ke lambe lambe baal dekho.

Oh dear, look at their strange ways, look at the long hair of the hippies.

From Shalimar Garden we went on to Pari Mahal and Ravi told me how it was built by the Mughal prince Dara Shikoh as his library. According to legend, the place was inhabited by fairies, and I remember asking Ravi many questions about their existence. At the entrance of the Chashm-e-Shahi gardens, Ravi treated me to an ice-cream cone.

Our next stop was Nehru Park, where we hired a shikara to take us to the middle of the Dal Lake. In chaste Kashmiri, the kind I had never heard Ravi speaking before, he bargained with the boatman. In the middle of the lake, when the waves hit the shikara making it sway a little, my heart sank. But I showed no fear. I didn't want Ravi to think of me as a sissy.

Back on Boulevard road, we went to a small eatery and Ravi bought us hot dogs. He also asked for a bottle of Gold Spot for me and a Thums Up for himself. He always had Thums Up.

On our way home, I urged him to speed up his bike, and he did so on some stretches. I was thrilled. I held him tightly.

For days afterwards, I would boast to my friends about Mendel, Dara Shikoh and the green-haired English mem I had seen.

Eleven years after that carefree day, the nightmare about Ravi I had had a few months earlier came true.

It was in September 1986 that Totha also left us. A few weeks prior to his death, on the day of Eid, he fell in his room and lost consciousness. After that, he was never able to stand on his feet. His reckless smoking had taken a toll on his lungs. His kidneys were also damaged because of excessive blood sugar. He was shifted to a bigger room on the first floor, and his bed lay beside a glass cabinet where Ravi kept his copies of *India Today*.

Totha was shocked by his new circumstances. He barely spoke, and for hours he would stare into nothingness. We visited him every day and tried to make him as comfortable as possible.

One day my aunt entered his room and found him smoking. She called my uncle and he admonished Totha for being so callous towards his condition. They searched his belongings and found a few cigarettes underneath his pillow. They were taken away. Throughout this episode, Totha did not utter a word. He kept his eyes closed.

A day later, I crossed over the dwarf fence to see him. He smiled weakly and I asked him to place his hands on the floor and I stepped onto them. He liked to get his hands pressed like this.

After a while, he looked at me and said, 'If I ask you to do something, will you do it?'

'Of course,' I said.

'Go to my room. Open the wooden trunk; you will find some money inside. Bring a ten-rupee note here to me,' he said.

I ran to his room and brought him the note.

'Now will you go and buy me two cigarettes from the shop? You can buy yourself a chocolate as well. But, listen, just get it discreetly, will you?'

Normally, I would have sprinted to the shop and got him what he wanted. But I remembered the previous day's episode. At the same time, I didn't want to blatantly say 'no' to him. With the note crumpled in my fist I stepped outside and then just sat on a stone slab beside a poplar tree. I waited for a while and then went back to Totha.

'Totha, no shop is open. There is some strike today,' I lied. Totha looked at me for several seconds. And then he said a feeble 'okay'.

'Keep the note with you, buy yourself whatever you want. And don't forget to share it with your sister,' he said.

I left, but I just couldn't bear the thought that I had lied to him. It was not that I had not lied to Totha before. Sometimes he would get me a present, and it wouldn't work properly. A pen, for example. After a few days he would ask me if I liked it, and I would invariably say 'yes'. But this time it was different.

I raced towards the market. I bought two Capstan cigarettes, the brand he usually smoked, and I brought them to him.

'Totha, I found the Fancy provision store open,' I said. He smiled. 'Just keep watch and alert me if someone comes up,' he said. I helped him sit up and put a cushion behind his back. He lit his cigarette while I kept watch at the head of the stairs. In between, I peeped in his room and saw him taking deep puffs.

His face looked peaceful. After he had finished, I threw the butt and the burnt matchstick out the window. Totha lay back on his bed. And then he mumbled a few lines from a Kashmiri verse about the birth of Krishna. When I was much younger, he would often sing that to me as a lullaby:

Gatte kani gash aav chaane zang'e
Jai, jai jai Devaki nandan'ey

On a moonless night, light spread on your accord
Salutations, O the beloved son of Devaki

A few days later, he passed away. He was cremated where Dedda and my grandfather had been cremated. In the garden that one could see through the window of his room, I built him a shrine and decorated it with marigold flowers and Mini chewing gum, which he had often bought for me.

A few months before his death, I had asked Totha to have his picture taken. Between Ravi's family and mine, we had many family albums. But there was not a single picture of Totha. After I had insisted for days, he agreed and had his picture taken with him wearing his trademark kurta and standing against the backdrop of the photographer's rainbow studio curtain.

After our exodus to Jammu, I searched for that photograph, hoping that it was among the few items we had managed to salvage before fleeing. But I didn't find it. In a way we were all thankful that barring my father's mother, no one from that generation had lived to experience the pain and difficulties of living in exile.

It was only a few years ago that I found Totha's picture inside some documents in my father's briefcase. It is now in my father's prayer room, along with pictures of my other ancestors.

〰

One summer night—it was 1988—we awoke to noises coming from the BSF camp behind our house. By the time I got up, my father and uncles were already on the rear balcony, looking in the direction of the camp. I joined them. My father asked me to remain quiet. From there, rubbing the sleep from my eyes, I saw a young man being beaten up by a few BSF soldiers. He lay on the road, and asked for water. But all he got was kick after kick. After some time, he was forced onto his feet and led into a building.

It was only the following morning when we learnt what had happened. The young man's name was Gowhar and he lived in a locality near ours. He was a karate expert and we kids adored him. Apparently, a few days earlier, he had had a tiff with a BSF soldier and punched him. Later, as he passed by the main gate of the BSF camp, the soldier and his friends accosted him and brought him inside where he was beaten up and kept in confinement. The next evening an angry crowd gathered outside the camp demanding his release. The BSF relented and he was set free.

I was doing my homework when I learnt that Gowhar had been set free and that he had been spotted eating a bagel at a local baker's. I rushed out to meet him and shake hands with him. He was our hero, having braved the kicks of those soldiers. But when I reached the bakery, he was not there. The baker didn't know where he had gone. I rushed to Latif's shop to find out if he knew about Gowhar's whereabouts. But his shop was closed.

I had been seeing less and less of Latif. His shop was either closed or manned by one of his friends or brothers. I asked Ravi about him. But he had no clue either. They had drifted apart a little. Ravi had been busy at the university, finishing his doctoral thesis. After graduating, he had been on the lookout for a job. Some of his friends had moved out of Kashmir to join private companies. But he did not want to leave.

It was around this time that my father had a mild heart attack. My father has always been prone to stomach ailments, and on that day he was in the office when he experienced severe pain in his abdomen. He was rushed to a gastroenterologist who recommended an injection for immediate relief. The injection caused a bad reaction—severe rashes broke out on his body and his speech turned incoherent.

It was always at such adverse moments that Ma would turn into a Joan of Arc. She was normally apprehensive. She didn't let me go for school picnics to the Aharbal waterfall for fear that someone might push me into it. During winters, when we sometimes accompanied Father on his official trips to Jammu, she would switch on her pencil torch the moment the bus entered the Jawahar tunnel, the only connection between the Kashmir Valley and the rest of India. During a storm she would close all the doors and windows and sit frightened in one corner, waiting for it to end. And if it lasted for long, she would look at Father and ask, 'Do you think this will end?'

Father would assure her a few times, but she would keep repeating her question till it irritated father.

'No, this is going to last till Doomsday.'

That day, she somehow gathered her nerves and accompanied Father to the *bod aspatal* (main hospital) in an autorickshaw.

The government hospital was crowded, and even in the emergency ward, it was difficult to find a doctor to attend to my father. As Ma ran from one counter to another, a young doctor appeared. There was a mark on his forehead, the result of offering namaz five times a day as is required of pious Muslims.

Ma recalled later how the doctor had looked at Father and immediately started his examination. And at that moment Father had vomited. It was so severe, Ma recalls, that it even filled the doctor's shoes. But not once did he flinch. He had continued to treat my father.

A day later, Father was back home, although it took him a couple of weeks to recover fully.

Life went on as usual. But around this time, something had begun to change. It was in the air, something you couldn't see, but could feel and smell.

Ma returned home one evening from office and she looked disconsolate. She entered slowly and set down her handbag. She asked my sister to get her some water. Father had come home early that day.

'Are you unwell?' he asked her.

She didn't speak for a moment or two. And then she narrated what she had witnessed. In the bus on her way home, a man had helped an old Pandit lady disembark from the bus. Another woman, who was a Muslim, lashed out at the man, reminding him that the woman he helped was a Pandit and that she should have instead been kicked out of the bus. What Ma witnessed that day in the bus, we considered an aberration.

Rehman, meanwhile, was acting strange at times. I remember we were getting our attic renovated and he took a dig at us.

'Why are you wasting your money like this?' he said as he poured milk from his can. 'Tomorrow, if not today, this house will belong to us.' As usual Ma dismissed his talk.

Ravi had gone on a plant-collection trip to the Lolab Valley along the Line of Control, with his department colleagues, including one of his best friends Irshad. In the forest they were waylaid by armed men who asked if there were any Hindus in their group. Ravi was the only one and the men were told that there were none. When they asked for their names, Ravi used a fake name that identified him as a Muslim. But, even then, we still didn't realize what was to come to pass.

On July 31, 1988, two low-intensity bomb blasts rocked Srinagar. One bomb had been planted outside the central telephone exchange while the other was laid outside the golf course. These were followed by other blasts. They were considered to be the handiwork of terrorists from Punjab who sneaked into Kashmir to escape the police in their area.

An uncle returned after praying at the Shankaracharya temple. 'I saw a group of men racing up and down the stairs,' he said. The same thing was happening at Hari Parbat. On the bypass road, near our house, even I saw hordes of men doing physical exercises. This had never happened before. It was only later that we realized that some of these men had been among those who had crossed over the border to Pakistan to receive arms training, and this had been a part of their fitness regimen.

A bomb blast in Srinagar claimed the first Pandit casualty in March 1989. Prabhawati of Chadoora tehsil was killed in a blast on Hari Singh Street on March 14. That month, I saw Latif one day. I was standing with Father at the vegetable shop when he passed by holding a corner of a green cloth which was held on the other corners by three others. He didn't see us. He was collecting funds, he said, for the building of a mosque.

I looked at him. He looked haggard, his skin was rugged and his beard thicker. It was then that his eyes fell on me and he smiled. He didn't look at Father. I didn't feel right in my heart.

The party walked on, holding their cloth.

It was from a neighbour that we heard the first rumours. He had gone to the ration shop to get sugar when he overheard a man exclaiming—'Inshallah, next ration we will buy in Islamabad!'

It was around this time that bus conductors in Lal Chowk could be heard shouting—*Sopore, Hand'wor, Upore.* Sopore and Handwara were border towns while *Upore* means across. Across the Line of Control. It was meant as an enticement for the youth to cross over the border for arms training, to launch a jihad against India.

On a hill in the Badami Bagh cantonment, someone had painted 'JKLF'. One could see it from a distance. It stood for Jammu and Kashmir Liberation Front. It was rumoured to be an organization of young men who had crossed over the border to receive arms training.

At school we heard the word 'mujahid' for the first time. We knew this word. We had heard it on TV, accompanied by images of men in Afghanistan firing rockets from their shoulders. But in the context of Kashmir, it seemed out of place. What were mujahids to do in Kashmir?

On June 23, 1989, pamphlets were distributed in Srinagar. It was an ultimatum to Muslim women, by an organization that called itself Hazb-i-Islami, to comply with 'Islamic' standards within two days or face 'action'. Pandit women were asked to put a tilak on their foreheads for identification.

On September 2, the 300-year-old Baba Reshi shrine was gutted in a fire under mysterious circumstances. On the same morning, a wireless operator of the Central Reserve Police Force (CRPF), was shot in our neighbourhood.

On the afternoon of September 14, I was playing cricket in the school grounds. My side won the match, and I was about to treat myself to an orange lolly with my pocket money when I felt someone's hand on my shoulder. I turned back and saw Father standing there. He smiled.

'Go and get your bag, we have to go home,' he said.

I thought something terrible had happened at home. 'Why, what happened?' I asked.

'Someone has been shot in Habba Kadal. The situation will turn worse. So we need to head home.'

That was when the first Pandit fell to bullets. Some armed men had entered the house of the political activist Tika Lal Taploo and shot him dead.

The next day, Father did not let me go to school. We were told that Taploo's funeral procession was pelted with stones. But barring that, nothing more untoward happened immediately after his death. I went back to school two days later. During the Hindi class, when the Muslim boys would be away for Urdu class, the Pandit teacher got an opportunity to discuss the killing with us. 'Times are beginning to get tough,' she said. 'That is why it is important for all of you to study with renewed vigour.'

In its preliminary investigation, the state police believed that Taploo's killing did not fit the pattern emerging from the activities of Kashmiri militants.

Twelve days after Taploo's death, the then chief minister, Farooq Abdullah, performed a small piece of classical dance along with dancer Yamini Krishnamurthy during a cultural function at the Martand temple. A few days later, he assured people that militancy would end soon.

On Eid-e-Milad-un-Nabi, on October 14, a massive crowd gathered near the Budshah chowk in the heart of Srinagar, and from there, it marched towards Eidgah to the graveyard that had been renamed the 'martyr's graveyard'. The onlookers cheered and showered *shireen* on the marchers as if to welcome a marriage procession. That evening, father returned home with a neighbour and they told us they had witnessed the procession. The crowd was shouting slogans that had shocked them.

Yahan kya chalega, Nizam-e-Mustafa
La sharqiya la garbiya, Islamia Islamia

What will work here? The rule of Mustafa
No eastern, no western, only Islamic, only Islamic

Zalzala aaya hai kufr ke maidaan mein,
Lo mujahid aa gaye maidaan mein

An earthquake has occurred in the realm of the infidels,
The mujahids have come out to fight

It was indeed an earthquake. It toppled everything in Kashmir in the next few weeks. Within a few days the whole scenario changed. There was another series of bomb blasts outside other symbols of 'Indianness'—India Coffee House, Punjab National Bank, the Press Trust of India. Then the tide turned against wine shops and cinema halls.

It was only much later that we were able to connect this turmoil to world events occurring around the same time. The Russians had withdrawn from Afghanistan nine years after they swept into the country. In Iran, Ayatollah Khomeini had urged Muslims to kill the author of *The Satanic Verses*. In Israel, a Palestinian bomber struck in a bus for the first time, killing sixteen civilians. A revolution was surging across Eastern Europe; and a bloodied frenzy was about to be unleashed against the Armenian Christian community in Azerbaijan.

In the midst of this chaos, my eldest uncle came from my father's village to visit us. 'The water in the spring at the goddess's sanctum has turned black,' he whispered. This was considered to be ominous. Legend had it that whenever any catastrophe befell our community, the spring waters turned black.

That it was indeed a catastrophe became clear on the night of January 19, 1990.

PART TWO

'*Kashmiriyon ki ragon mein Mujahideen aur ghaziyon ka khoon hai . . .*' (In the veins of Kashmiris flows the blood of the Mujahideen and the destructors of the infidels . . .)

Her face quivers as she shouts at the top of her voice, and her dupatta keeps slipping down. But her lipstick remains intact. It is her moment, undoubtedly. With every drop of bile coming from Benazir Bhutto's mouth, the mammoth crowd's cheers grow noisier until they turn into a stormy sea. And her voice runs like a tide over it. Her rabidness is a Godzilla.

'*Har eik gaanv se eik hi aawaz buland hogi: Azadi! Har eik masjid se eik hi aawaz buland hogi: Azadi! Har eik school se baccha-baccha kahega: Azadi, Azadi, Azadi!*'

(From every village will rise a cry: Azadi! From every mosque will rise a cry: Azadi! From every school, every child will let out the cry: Azadi, Azadi, Azadi!)

It is 1990, seventeen years before Benazir's ghazis would end up devouring her.

In one giant leap, it hops over from Islamabad to Kashmir. And it manifests itself in the house of a Pandit in Budgam district. Bhushan Lal Raina lives with his mother in Budgam's Ompora area and works at the Soura Medical Institute. The developments in Srinagar have scared him and he wants to escape to Jammu. A day before he is to leave, armed men barge into his house. Raina's old mother begs them to spare her son. 'He is about to get married; kill me if you want, but spare him,' she implores. But the ghazis won't listen. One of them pierces

Raina's skull with an iron rod. Then they drag him out, strip him, and nail him to a tree.

Throughout 1990, Pandits are picked up selectively and put to death. They are killed because Kashmir needs to be cleansed of them. And if the one chosen is not to be found, a proxy suffices. It is all about numbers. It is all about how many are killed. It is known that if one among them is killed, a thousand will flee.

But we were fools. Though we knew something was afoot, we refused to believe that our turn would come soon.

Not very far from where Bhushan Lal Raina was killed in front of his mother, Mohan Lal leaves his home as usual one evening. He is a simple man and does odd jobs to sustain his family. Among the three Hindu families of his village, his house is just a structure of bricks, and every winter, its tin roof caves in after heavy snowfall. He often ventures out in the evening; he likes to sit outside the house of another Pandit family who are well off and own several orchards. There is a large garden in front of the house, in which the lady of the house dries chillies and patties of special Kashmiri spices.

That winter evening in 1990, the lady sits alone in her house, waiting for her husband to return. Mohan Lal sits outside. He has a habit of repeatedly looking at his watch and asking passers-by what time it is. Two men clad in pherans throw a cursory glance at him and enter the house.

'Where is your husband?' one of them asks the lady inside.

'He is not here; he will come tomorrow,' she replies. She senses that the men do not mean well. She lies to them about her husband's arrival.

The men look at each other and leave without saying another word. They come out and find Mohan Lal still there. One of them whips out a gun and shoots him dead. Mohan Lal falls down with his mouth open, one hand clenching his wristwatch.

The guns are never silenced after the September of 1989. Every day, news pours in of attacks on military convoys or bunkers. Srinagar city turns into a war zone. Armed men exchange fire with paramilitary forces and many civilians are caught in the crossfire.

Once the Pandits have left, novel methods are used to alert people of an impending ambush in the marketplace. The militant commander Mushtaq Zargar—he hits international headlines ten years later as one of the three men India is forced to free in exchange for the hostages of the hijacked flight IC-814—sends vegetable vendors to such places. Pushing his cart, the vendor shouts in Kashmiri: *Tamatar paav, Bae'jaan aav* (Tomatoes, one-fourth of a kilo, big brother says hello). While the soldiers from the mainland of India understand nothing, civilians take the hint and discreetly vacate the area to avoid being caught in the crossfire.

But for the Pandits, there is no such concern. For the Ghazis invoked by Benazir Bhutto, we are infidels. And we deserve to die.

In October 1989, we still didn't know.

On October 31, the militant commander Hamid Sheikh is critically injured in an encounter with military personnel. He is among the first groups of men to have crossed the Line of Control in 1988 to undergo arms training. By 1989–90, thousands of boys have followed his example.

By October, a few other Pandits have been killed. Retired judge Neelkanth Ganjoo is waylaid by three men on Hari Singh Street, in the heart of Srinagar, and shot at close range. His body remains there untouched for fifteen minutes. Later, the police arrives and takes his body away.

On December 6, 1989, exactly three years before the demolition of the Babri Masjid created a deep laceration in Indian society, a Kashmiri politician was unexpectedly appointed Union home minister by the central government in Delhi. Mufti Mohammed Sayeed, whose political career began with the Congress party, is someone whom the Pandits hold responsible for the 1986 Anantnag riots.

Two days after Sayeed took over, armed youths kidnapped his daughter Rubaiya from a minibus as she returned from the Lal Ded hospital, where she worked as a doctor. The militants demanded the release of five imprisoned men in exchange for Rubaiya. These five were part of the first batch of men who had crossed the Line of Control to receive arms training.

Kashmir was like a deer's neck in a wolf's grip.

Eight days later, five militants were released in downtown Srinagar to secure Rubaiya's release. One of them was Hamid Sheikh. On the morning he was to be released from the Soura Medical Institute, a photographer from a local newspaper asked him to pose for a picture. He did it happily, flashing a victory sign. I couldn't help noticing that on a table behind him there was a tin of Cinthol talcum powder. From 3 p.m. onwards, celebrations began in the Kashmir Valley. Lal Chowk was lined with JKLF flags. A throng of people assembled at Hamid

Sheikh's house in Batmaloo. Candy was showered and women sang songs traditionally sung to welcome a bridegroom. There was celebratory gunfire in many places. In Shopian, in south Kashmir, a mob came out and beat up Pandit men on the streets. Scores of women were molested to make merry. Shortly afterwards, militants issued a diktat to newsreaders to quit their jobs in radio and television so that the government information mechanism would collapse.

January 19, 1990, was a very cold day despite the sun's weak attempts to emerge from behind dark clouds. In the afternoon, I played cricket with some boys from my neighbourhood. All of us wore thick sweaters and pherans. I would always remove my pheran and place it on the fence in the kitchen garden. After playing, I would wear it before entering the house to escape my mother's wrath. She worried that I would catch cold. 'The neighbours will think that I am incapable of taking care of my children,' she would say in exasperation.

We had an early dinner that evening and, since there was no electricity, we couldn't watch television. Father heard the evening news bulletin on the radio as usual, and just as we were going to sleep, the electricity returned.

I am in a deep slumber. I can hear strange noises. Fear grips me. All is not well. Everything is going to change. I see shadows of men slithering along our compound wall. And then they jump inside. One by one. So many of them.

I woke up startled. But the zero-watt bulb was not on. The hundred-watt bulb was. Father was waking me up. 'Something is happening,' he said. I could hear it—there were people out on the streets. They were talking loudly. Some major activity was underfoot. Were they setting our locality on fire?

So, it wasn't entirely a dream, after all? Will they jump inside now?

Then a whistling sound could be heard. It was the sound of the mosque's loudspeaker. We heard it every day in the wee hours of the morning just before the muezzin broke into the azaan. But normally the whistle was short-lived; that night, it refused to stop. That night, the muezzin didn't call. That night, it felt like something sinister was going to happen.

The noise outside our house had died down. But in the mosque, we could hear people's voices. They were arguing about something.

My uncle's family came to our side of the house. 'What is happening?' Uncle asked. 'Something is happening,' Father said. 'They are up to something.'

It was then that a long drawl tore through the murmurs, and with the same force the loudspeaker began to hiss.

'*Naara-e-taqbeer, Allah ho Akbar!*'

I looked at my father; his face was contorted. He knew only too well what the phrase meant. I had heard it as well, in a stirring drama telecast a few years ago on Doordarshan, an adaptation of Bhisham Sahni's *Tamas*, a novel based on the events of the 1947 partition of India and Pakistan. It was the cry that a mob of Muslim rioters shouted as it descended upon Hindu settlements. It was a war cry.

Within a few minutes, battle cries flew at us from every direction. They rushed towards us like poison darts.

Hum kya chaaaahte: Azadiiii!
Eiy zalimon, eiy kafiron, Kashmir humara chhod do.

What do we want—Freedom!
O tyrants, O infidels, leave our Kashmir.

Then the slogans ceased for a while. From another mosque came the sound of recorded songs eulogizing the Mujahideen resistance to the Soviet occupation of Afghanistan. The whole audio cassette played through, and then the slogans returned. We were still wondering what would happen next when a slogan we heard left us in no doubt. I remember Ma began to tremble like a leaf when we heard it.

'*Assi gacchi panu'nuy Pakistan, batav rostuy, batenein saan.*'

The crowd wanted to turn Kashmir into Pakistan, without the Pandit men, but with their women.

They'll come and finish us. It is just a matter of minutes now, we think.

Ma rushed to the kitchen and returned with a long knife. It was her father's. 'If they come, I will kill her,' she looked at my sister. 'And then I will kill myself. And you see what you two need to do.'

Father looked at her in disbelief. But he didn't utter a word.

We are very scared. We do not know what to do. Where would we run away to? Would Ma have to kill herself? What about my sister?

My life flashed in front of me, like a silent film. I remembered my childhood with my sister. How I played with her and how she always liked to play 'teacher-teacher', making me learn the spellings of 'difficult' words.

B-E-A-U-T-I-F-U-L
T-O-R-T-O-I-S-E
F-E-B-R-U-A-R-Y
C-H-R-I-S-T-M-A-S
P-O-R-C-U-P-I-N-E

I remembered the red ribbon she wore; I remembered how she waited behind the closed gates of her school to catch a glimpse of father's shoes from beneath; I remembered how she threw a duster at one of her friends who tried to bully me; I remembered how I left her alone in the middle of a game of hopscotch because I saw Ravi's mother entering the house with a parrot in a cage. *Would Mother stab her? And herself? What would we do?*

'The BSF will do something,' Uncle said. But nobody does anything. The slogan-mongering continued all night. We could see searchlights from somewhere making an arc over and over again. Was the BSF keeping a watch? Why were they not stopping this madness?

The slogans did not stop till the early hours of the morning. We remained awake the whole night. As the first rays of the sun broke, I dozed off for a while and when I woke up everyone was still there. Ma was still holding on to the knife.

The crowd took a break in the morning. I don't think we had ever been as happy as we were when dawn broke that day. It gave us an elemental sense of hope, of security.

It was later that we realized that it was not only in our locality that this had happened. These incidents had occured all over the Kashmir Valley at around the same time. It was well orchestrated. It was meant to frighten us into exile.

Three hundred kilometres away, in a former palace, a man spent that night feeling absolutely helpless. Jagmohan had been sent by New Delhi to take charge as the governor of Jammu and Kashmir. On the afternoon of January 19, he had boarded a BSF plane that had brought him to Jammu. While being driven to the Raj Bhavan, he saw people lining up on both sides of the road to greet him. Jagmohan was a very popular administrator and, during a previous stint in 1986 as the governor of the state, he had won the hearts of the people by undertaking large-scale reforms. That night in Jammu's Raj Bhavan, the phone began to ring from 10 p.m. onwards. 'They are coming to kill us,' a scared Pandit from somewhere in the Valley whispered to him. 'Please ask the army to help us,' begged another. But that night, Jagmohan was not in a position to help them at all. The administration, he knew, had collapsed completely. Some sections of the police were sympathetic to militant groups. No one was in charge. And as usual, in New Delhi, the babus in the government had no idea what was happening. On Doordarshan, as Jagmohan would recount in his memoirs later, a special programme on the 'ethnic revolt' in Azerbaijan was being telecast. Only a week earlier, in the Azerbaijani capital of Baku, a massive crowd demanding independence from Soviet Russia had attacked the Christian Armenian community, killing hundreds in a bloodied frenzy, and looting their homes and business establishments. And oblivious to New Delhi, a similar episode was about to occur in Kashmir.

Only the gods could save the Pandits now.

The next morning, the exodus began. Families stuffed whatever little they could into a few suitcases and slipped away to Jammu. In some places, we later learnt, people had suffered worse than us the previous night.

At Draebyaar, Habba Kadal, for hours stones had been showered over Pandit houses. In several places, families were threatened. 'Bring petrol, let's burn them down!' someone had shouted outside the house of father's colleague in Jawahar Nagar. The next morning the family left, leaving the house keys with their Muslim neighbours.

Sometimes I think back to the events of the night of January 19. How does one depict the fear we felt that night? I found my answer much later in Art Spiegelman's *Maus*, a graphic novel in which the author interviews his father, a holocaust survivor. Depicting the Jews as mice and the Nazis as cats, Spiegelman asks his father how it felt to be in the Auschwitz concentration camp. His father startles him by producing a loud 'Boo!' and says 'it felt a little like that. But always!' That is how we felt on the night of January 19.

Two days later, a massive procession began from our locality to Jama Masjid in downtown Srinagar. The crowd was demanding azadi. One of our Muslim neighbour's sons was very young, not a day older than three, and he had curly brown hair. That day he went missing. A frantic search was launched for him but he was nowhere to be found. Later in the day, one of the family's acquaintances reported that the boy had followed a few older boys to downtown Srinagar to take part in the procession. Four days later, on January 25, four unarmed personnel of the Indian Air Force were gunned down near our house. It was about 8 a.m. and the men were waiting for their bus when gunmen riding on motorcycles sprayed them with bullets. One of the dead was a squadron leader.

The slogans and the war cries from the mosque did not stop. So, in a way, every day in Kashmir after January 19 was January 19. The cries just became a little more systematic. They would begin during the night and continue till the wee hours of the morning. After a break, they would resume until late morning. Then another break and so it would go on.

Processions would stream into Srinagar from all over. There were several instances of Pandits being forced out of their homes to lead such processions. This was done to ensure that in case the paramilitary charged at the crowd or fired at it, the Pandits would become the first targets.

Initially, the first few killings of Pandits were carried out quite surgically. But as the euphoria reached its zenith, the killings turned more macabre. On February 2, a young Pandit businessman named Satish Tickoo was called out of his home by a few men and shot at point-blank range. Tickoo knew them. One of them lived nearby and often took lifts from Tickoo on his scooter. When the man whipped out a pistol, Tickoo tried to save himself by hurling his kangri at the assailants. But it missed them. The first bullet hit him in his jaw. As he fell down, the men pumped several more into his body.

Tickoo's main assailant, the same man who often rode with him on his scooter, was identified as Farooq Ahmad Dar alias Bitta Karate. He was arrested in June that year. In a TV interview shortly afterwards, he confessed that he had killed twenty people, most of them Kashmiri Pandits and that his first kill was Tickoo. Here's an excerpt from that interview:

Journalist: How many people did you kill?

Karate: I don't remember.

Journalist: So you killed so many people that you don't even remember?

Karate: Ten to twelve I must have killed.

Journalist: Ten to twelve or twenty?

Karate: You can say twenty.

Journalist: Were all of them Kashmiri Pandits? Or were there some Muslims as well?

Karate: Some Muslims as well.

Journalist: How many Muslims and how many Pandits?

[Silence . . .]

Journalist: So there were more Kashmiri Pandits?

Karate: Yes.

Journalist: But why so?

Karate: We had orders.

Journalist: Who was the first person you killed?

[Long silence . . .]

Journalist: When did you commit your first murder?

Karate: Let me think. First murder I committed was of Satish.

Journalist: Satish who?

Karate: Satish Kumar Tickoo.

Journalist: Satish Kumar Tickoo! Who was he?

Karate: I got the order from the higher up to hit him and I did that.

Journalist: Who was he?

Karate: A Pandit boy.

Though Karate spent sixteen years in jail, he was not convicted. While releasing him on bail the judge remarked:

> The court is aware of the fact that the allegations levelled against the accused are of serious nature and carry a punishment of death sentence or life imprisonment but the fact is that the prosecution has shown total disinterest in arguing the case, which is in complete violation of Article 21 of the Constitution.

Karate's case is not an outlier. In hundreds of cases of Pandit killings, not a single person was convicted. Karate has returned to normal life and has since married and become a father. In a sparse room in Jammu, on the other hand, Prithvi Nath Tickoo looks at a photograph of his son and tears well up in his eyes. 'He (Satish) had an inkling that something would happen,' he recalls. The father–son duo ran a medical agency. Just before he was killed, Satish had told his father that they should shift to Jammu. 'But to avoid arousing suspicion that we were leaving, he said we shall shift our belongings gradually,' Prithvi Nath Tickoo says. After they shifted to Jammu, the Tickoos finally sold their house for peanuts. 'My house was three-storeyed and it had forty-seven windows,' remembers the senior Tickoo inhaling the stale air of his windowless room.

On the morning of February 8, I was studying at home when I heard a loud noise, as if a building had collapsed. Then there was absolute silence. We came out onto the veranda, not sure whether we should venture out further. 'I think there has been a heavy burst of firing somewhere nearby,' father said. One of our neighbours came out on to the street and she was crying. Her son was out and she was worried about him. But, thankfully, he returned soon afterwards. He had been at the milkman's shop buying curd, when all of a sudden there was firing followed by complete chaos. He dropped the steel pitcher he was carrying and ran away.

In a few moments, the entire locality was surrounded by BSF soldiers. A soldier positioned himself just outside our house. We climbed up to the roof to get a better view. The soldier saw us and asked us to go inside. We learnt that two BSF soldiers buying vegetables at a shop had been shot dead. The gunfire had come from the temple opposite the shop, and it had also killed the milkman from whose shop our neighbours' son had bought curd. I knew that milkman very well. Sometimes, in the

severe cold, when curd wouldn't set, I, like my neighbour, would
be sent to fetch some from him.

A day later I went to the scene of the incident with a friend to
have a look. All the shops were closed. Outside the vegetable
shop, bloodstains were clearly visible. A few onions lay strewn
on the ground.

On the night of February 13, we learnt about yet another
death, this time of Doordarshan Kashmir's director, Lassa Kaul.
The Kauls were known to my father—he knew that Kaul came
from a humble background, and had, through sheer grit and
determination, made it to the prestigious post. In the past few
weeks, Kaul had been finding it difficult to continue working
amidst threats. This had made him move, two days prior to his
murder, to a guarded government accommodation. On the
night of his murder, he had visited his house in Bemina to meet
his handicapped father who lived there alone. An investigation
conducted after his death indicated that information about his
movements may have been leaked to the militants by one of
his colleagues.

For days Father could not believe that Kaul was no more and
that he had met such a brutal end.

I often think of those days, and I realize how Father kept
deferring our departure even after the signs of what was to
become of us were so clear. I think it was mainly because of the
house he had built after so much struggle—the house that was
our home, the house that had twenty-two rooms.

On February 22 of that year, we celebrated our last Shivratri at
home. That year, we did not go to Habba Kadal to buy fish or

earthenware. There was too much grief. And fear. Ma hastily cooked a meal and we performed pooja silently. We were so scared, Father did not blow our ancestral conch as he had always done, to welcome the arrival of Lord Shiva.

One of the Pandit leaders, H.N. Jattu, wrote an open letter to the JKLF, asking them to make their stand on the Kashmiri Pandits clear. The JKLF took it seriously and responded the next day.

The second day of Shivratri was one of the coldest that season. It had snowed heavily and the snow had frozen on the roads, making it quite difficult to commute. But in that weather, hundreds of buses carrying thousands of people were out in procession. The rooftops of the buses were crowded with men wearing shrouds to indicate that they were ready to die for the cause of freedom. They were on their way to the Charar-e-Sharif shrine, where the Sufi saint Nund Rishi (or *Nund Bab*), revered by both Hindus and Muslims, was laid to rest after his death in 1438. En route, wherever they came across a Pandit, they would hurl abuses at him. Many winked and made obscene gestures at women. In Tankipora, one of Jattu's close associates, Ashok Kumar Qazi, was accosted by three armed men. While two men held him, another shot him in his knees. As he collapsed on the road, they kicked him, making him fall into a drain. One man unzipped his trousers and sprayed piss over him. As he writhed in pain, the men fired a few more shots and killed him. His killing was the JKLF's answer to H.N. Jattu's letter.

The news affected my father badly. He had known the Qazi family well. In fact, one of Ashok's brothers lived near our house. Two days later, Father went quietly to the Doodh Ganga river behind our house and bid farewell to the gods. It was like Shiva had eloped with his bride. There was no joy, no festivity.

On the evening of February 27, Naveen Sapru left his office as usual. The thirty-seven-year-old telecom department employee boarded a minibus for Habba Kadal, as he wanted to collect his coat from a tailor first. In Habba Kadal, at a mosque, a few men had gathered hours before, making plans to eliminate him. They had been tracking his movements for days. As he reached the Habba Kadal bridge, they caught hold of Sapru. They shot him. His attackers surrounded him and, joined by many others, they danced around him. An old Pandit woman who happened to pass by begged his assailants to spare him. But they abused her and one of them pushed her away. As he lay there, his life ebbing out of him, a few from the crowd threw *shireen* at him as is done over a corpse. Minutes later, Navin Sapru bled to death.

When a police truck arrived and took his body to the cremation ground, the crowd followed it cheering from behind and shouting slogans.

Navin Sapru's friend, the poet and writer Maharaj Krishan Santoshi, wrote a poem on his death. In 'Naveen my friend', Santoshi writes:

> Naveen was my friend
> Killed he was, in Habba Kadal
> while on the tailor's hanger remained hung
> his warm coat.
> Passing as it did through scissors and thread–needle
> in the tailor's hand, till the previous day
> it was merely a person's coat
> that suddenly was turned into a Hindu's coat

In the last stanza the poet writes:

> I used to ask him every time
> why doesn't he possess the cunningness of Srinagar

I still await his response
My friend! Yes, I changed my address
since after your murder
it ceased to exist
the bridge of friendship, this Habba Kadal

The assault from the mosques continued all this while. We spent most of our time locked inside, venturing out only to buy vegetables and other daily necessities. By this time, curfew had become the norm due to the deteriorating law and order situation. Whenever curfew was lifted, Father and Ma would have to go to work.

On the morning of March 7, I was playing in the compound of our house. It must have been around 10 a.m., and Father and Ma had left for office. Suddenly, I heard the distinctive sound of gunfire. It rent the air and the pigeons in our attic took flight in alarm. I froze. The sound had been quite loud. Something had happened nearby. In a few minutes, a minibus owned by one of our Muslim neighbours raced up the street. That meant something had gone terribly wrong. A little later Father returned as well. He was fumbling for words.

'Has your mother returned?' he asked. I replied in the negative.

'There has been heavy firing,' he said.

After Father had left with Ma, she had taken a bus upon spotting a colleague in it. Father was worried since the firing had taken place near her destination.

We waited for a while. But Ma did not return. One of our neighbours said that two soldiers had died in the firing and many were injured. There had been a heavy exchange of fire.

This worried Father even more. He rushed to our neighbour Nehvi Uncle's house. Though he did not share his fears with me, I knew exactly what was going through father's mind. He feared that Ma was one of the victims of the firing. Along with Nehvi Uncle, father rushed to the bone-and-joint hospital in Barzulla where the injured had been admitted for treatment. They looked everywhere, but Ma was not there. They returned home.

An hour or so later, Ma returned. A cry of relief escaped father's lips when he saw her. She was walking slowly and her lips were trembling. She sat on the veranda and asked for some water. We were overjoyed that she was unharmed. After she had caught her breath, Ma told us what had happened. Just as she had got off the bus, bullets started to fly. She saw a man get hit in his abdomen, and blood oozing out of it. Everyone ran helter-skelter. She ran and hid behind a shop. Afterwards, she began to walk through the fields towards our home. But she lost her way. And then she saw Latif. He saw her as well, and without exchanging a word, he held her arm and guided her through the fields. After some time they came to the main road where a group of soldiers was patrolling. Upon spotting them, Latif slipped away. But Ma was safe. From there on she knew the way home.

'But I don't understand why Latif ran away,' she said after a while.

We were silent. Father probably knew. And in my heart I knew as well. But I did not think too much about it. I was just happy that my mother was safe.

A day later, a multi-party political delegation led by the former prime minister Rajiv Gandhi arrived in Kashmir to take stock of the situation. But the former prime minister had arrived with the sole purpose of creating an unnecessary fuss. Upon landing in Srinagar airport, Rajiv Gandhi immediately expressed displeasure over Governor Jagmohan's not coming to the airport to receive the deputy prime minister, Devi Lal. Jagmohan said he had not been told about Devi Lal's arrival. Later Gandhi complained that Devi Lal was made to sit on the left side of the governor, which was apparently against protocol. The delegation, which included stalwarts like George Fernandes and Harkishan Singh Surjeet, skipped Jammu altogether to escape the wrath of the Pandits who had already fled their homes and were now refugees in their own country.

A veteran communist leader, Reshi Dev, who was a Kashmiri Pandit, apprised Surjeet of the situation and asked him to raise his voice against the brutality that had been unleashed against the Pandit community. '*Aisee baatein chalti rehti hein*—such things keep on happening,' he shot back.

We were already becoming nobody's people.

Shortly afterwards, we slipped away from home one morning and took refuge in my mother's sister's house. Her family lived near the army cantonment, and it was safe there. Father spent the day listening to news bulletins. But the state radio and television carried no news reports. It was only BBC Radio that gave the correct picture. From the news reports, it was clear that the situation in the Valley had spiralled beyond control.

After a week or so, Father grew restless and wanted to return home. So we left my sister behind, and the three of us returned late one afternoon.

The whole neighbourhood had moved out. The entire locality was deserted. The Razdans had left, so had the Bhans, and the

Mattoos. It looked like a ghost street. Not a soul was to be seen anywhere. We slipped inside our house like robbers. We walked past the kitchen garden, frost-ridden and barren, and entered the house through a side door. Then Father made sure the main door was locked so if somebody were to check, he would think the house was vacant, like every other house in the locality. Father instructed us not to switch on any lights and to keep the curtains drawn across the windows. He also urged us to speak in hushed tones. To feel a little more secure, Father had asked one of his staff members, Satish, to come and stay with us. Satish had married recently, and Father and I had attended his wedding in Budgam. Satish had made his family move to Jammu. His government job had been hard to come by and he was not sure if he would be able to keep it were he to move to Jammu, so he stayed behind.

We just sat there in a room upstairs and talked about the situation. Satish spoke about how Pandits were being killed all across the Valley.

Suddenly, we hear laughter outside. Then someone passes a remark and there is the sound of laughter again. Father goes to the window and after taking a deep breath lifts the corner of the curtain to look outside. I kneel on the ground near him and peep outside as well. Near the main gate below, there is a gang of boys. Some of them are smoking. I know most of them. They are boys from our neighbourhood—near and far—and I have played cricket with some of them. Their ringleader is a boy who lives nearby. 'He is even trained in rocket launchers,' one of them says loudly, boasting about his cousin who is with a militant group now.

'Let's distribute these houses,' one of them shouts. 'Akram, which one do you want?' he asks.

'I would settle for this house any day,' he points to a house.

'Bastard,' shoots back another, 'how you wish you could occupy this house with their daughter!'

There is a peal of laughter. They make obscene gestures with their fists and Akram pretends as if he is raping the girl and is now close to an orgasm. Since I am kneeling next to Father, from the corner of my left eye, I can see that his legs have begun to shake.

In the next few minutes, all of them have one house each. In between they discuss other girls. And then Akram asks the ringleader, 'Hey Khoja, you haven't specified your choice!'

The ringleader is wearing a pheran and there is a cricket bat in his hands. He is smoking. He savours the question for a moment. Everybody is looking at him now. The ringleader then turns and now he is facing our gate. He lifts his arm, and points his finger towards it. He lets it stay afloat in the air for a moment and then he says it.

'I will take this!'

The corner of the curtain drops from Father's grip. He crumbles to the floor right there. He closes his eyes and is shaking. I think I hear someone from the gang shouting: 'Good choice, baaya, good choice.'

Then it all blanks out. I can hear nothing more. There is a buzzing sound in my ear, as if my cochlea has burst. One of them must have then picked up a stone and thrown it at Razdan's house. The sound of glass breaking tears through the freezing air. Pigeons take flight. A pack of dogs begins to bark.

'Haya kyoho goy,' says one of them, 'you have incurred losses upon Akram. Now he will have to replace this windowpane.'

'At least go inside and piss; like a dog you need to mark your territory.'

And then they leave. Their voices grow distant till they completely fade away. Silence prevails again except for the staccato barking of mongrels and the cooing of pigeons that are returning to the attic.

'It's over,' Father said. 'We cannot live here anymore.'

Ma went to the storeroom and fetched a few candles that she always kept handy. In candlelight, she made turmeric rice. There was neither will nor appetite for an elaborate dinner. We ate silently, and quite early. I was so stressed that my stomach was in knots. Satish was feeling cold and Father told him to take one of his sweaters from our huge wooden wardrobe. I went with him. While he looked for the sweater, he nervously took a crumpled cigarette from his trouser pocket, lit it, and pulled so deep that the cigarette finished in three or four drags. After he left the room, I picked up the cigarette butt and lit it again till the filter burnt. I was nervous and thought a few puffs would calm me down.

Father told us we would have to leave early the next morning. That night we couldn't sleep. We just lay beneath our quilts and Ma kept her torch beside her as usual. Father spoke to Satish in hushed tones. In the middle of the night we heard a thud as if someone had jumped from the boundary wall into our compound. It turned out to be a false alarm—a pigeon had pushed a loose brick from the attic on to the ground.

Early in the morning, it had begun to snow. There was snow already on the roads and some of it had turned into slush. Father said he would first venture out and see if it was safe for us to leave. I held his hand and both of us came out onto the street. Father closed the gate very softly behind us. Suddenly, a bearded man wearing a thick jacket appeared on the other side of the street. His pockets were bulging. His eyes fell on us and Father fumbled. His grip on my hand tightened and we turned back. Father pretended as if he had forgotten something inside the house. We hurried in, with Father locking every door behind him.

After a while, we came out again. At the main gate, painted blue, Father saw a piece of paper that had been stuck onto it. It was a hit list. Written in Urdu, with 'JKLF' across the top, it warned the Pandits to leave the Valley immediately. A list of about ten people followed—the list of people who the JKLF said would be killed.

I read some of the names. Some of them were of our neighbours. 'We must tell Kaul sa'eb about it,' Father said. Together, we almost ran to his house.

'I hope nobody sees us,' Father muttered.

The previous evening, we had seen our neighbour, Mr Kaul, at the bus stop. Father and he had got talking and Mr Kaul had said he was going to stay put.

'Pandita sa'eb, you don't worry. The army has come now, and it will all be over in a couple of months,' he had said.

At the Kaul residence the first thing I noticed was that the evergreen shrubs that had not been tended for weeks now. The main gate was open and we entered. We found the main door locked.

'Maybe they are inside,' Father said. Very hesitantly, he called out Kaul sa'eb's name. There was no response. The Kauls had left already. We hurriedly turned back. Satish and my mother were waiting. Ma had packed whatever she could. And we left immediately.

At the blue gate, Father stopped and turned back. He looked at the house. Looking back, there was a sense of finality in his gaze. There were tears in his eyes. Ma was calm. Satish stood next to me. Nobody uttered a word. Before we moved on, Father recited something that I remember well. The howling of a dog near one's house was believed to be a bad omen. So if it happened, the occupants uttered: *Yetti gach, yeti chhuy ghar divta* (Leave from here, O misfortune, this house is guarded by the deity of the house).

Satish went back to his house to try and salvage whatever he could. He had also decided overnight to join his family in Jammu.

As we walked to the bus stop, we found all the shops closed. There were hardly any people on the road. Although the curfew had been relaxed for a few hours that day, there was not much traffic.

We got into a minibus and reached Lal Chowk. Ma had removed the golden *atth* from her ears and her bindi that identified her as a Pandit. Father removed the red sacred thread from his wrist. At Lal Chowk, Father managed to convince an autorickshaw driver to drop us to the outskirts of the cantonment, from where we could walk to the safety of my mother's sister's house.

En route, we saw that the army had taken over. Jawans had built bunkers on the road and inside various buildings. By the time we reached my aunt's house, my feet were frozen so badly I thought they might have to be amputated. I removed my wet socks and a cry escaped my lips when I put my feet up on the kangri. My sister was happy we were back. Everyone had been worried.

The news was not good. Advertisements had appeared in some Urdu newspapers. Released by various militant organizations, they asked the Pandits to leave the Valley immediately or face dire consequences.

I passed the next few weeks in a daze. There was complete uncertainty about our future. There was madness on the streets outside. Every day, someone or the other would be gunned down. Even at my aunt's house, we were under a house arrest of sorts.

I can't fathom why all this is happening. If the Kashmiris are demanding Azadi, why do the Pandits have to be killed? Why do we have to leave our house, where I play freely, and ride my cycle, and exchange comics with my friends? How is the burning of a temple or molesting a Pandit lady on the road going to help in the cause of Azadi?

During those nerve-wracking days, the only thing we looked forward to was the evening news bulletin on the Kashmir Doordarshan channel. Bereft of its experienced news anchors, Doordarshan had hired a bunch of inexperienced presenters to read the news. The news they offered was hardly reliable. But in those unfortunate days, they provided us with moments of laughter. At 7.30 p.m., the news would be announced and the presenter would appear on the television screen, still waiting for his cue. He would stare at the camera for a few seconds and then read the news like a stuttering duck. In between, he would stop and, sometimes in his nervousness, forget that he was live on television. He would then gesture to the cameraman or the producer, seeking directions.

We children compared these presenters to a brilliant Kashmiri comedian who in the mid eighties had kept us glued to the television with the two roles he played. In one, he played the part of a weird, autocratic king who would have to be hit with a royal hammer to bring him back to his senses after which he would ask for water in such a funny way that we would mimic him for months in school. After our exodus, we heard rumours of his death in a road accident. But I was both happy and relieved to watch him perform in a festival in Delhi a few years ago.

'We cannot stay like this any longer,' Father said one day. 'We need to leave, we need to put you in a school.'

For the last few days, Father had been watching me and my sister and it had set him thinking. My sister was in college. I would take out my books every morning, but for the rest of the day I would simply flit from room to room, play cricket, or read comic books when it was too cold to venture outside.

It was quite sunny the day Father finally decided that we should move to Jammu. He had spoken to a colleague who had promised to help. He arranged a taxi to take us to Jammu, and advised us not to tell the driver that we were leaving permanently. There had been reports at various places that mobs had beaten up fleeing families and looted their belongings. In one instance a family had called a truck to load their possessions to escape to Jammu, but at the last moment a mob had descended and lynched them and then taken away every article the family possessed.

In our case it was not so difficult. We had hardly any luggage to arouse suspicion. And though Father had left our house with a sense of finality, somewhere in his heart I think he still liked to believe what many of us did at that time—that this would be over sooner or later.

The taxi arrived the following morning. All we had was a small bag and two suitcases. And my school bag. The driver was told that we were off to Jammu to attend a wedding. As he was putting our luggage in the boot of his Ambassador car, the driver looked at my school bag and smiled. 'Pandit ji, I know you people lay a lot of emphasis on education, but at least let this kid have fun for a week.'

The driver turned his key in the ignition and we began our journey. 'We'll be back soon,' Mother shouted to her sister. It was quiet in the car. Father sat in front and I sat behind with my mother and sister. Both of them had covered their heads with a dupatta.

'We need to beat the army convoys on the highway, otherwise we will be stuck for a long time,' the driver said. On the highway, by the shops, men stood huddled. At some places there were tyres smouldering in the frost. A little further ahead, we could see the ruins of the Martand sun temple.

We drove on silently. Eventually, we had to slow down to give way to oncoming vehicles on a narrow stretch of road. Suddenly a man appeared from nowhere. He was pushing a small wheelbarrow. He looked at us and pumped his fist in the air. He shouted: '*Maryu, Batav, maryu!*' (Die, you Pandits, die!)

We were scared. The driver said nothing. He kept looking ahead as if he had not heard anything, as if the man did not exist, as if his fist did not exist, as if his voice did not exist.

As if we did not exist in his taxi.

Travelling on the highway had always been a pleasurable experience. Every winter, we would take this road to Jammu and stay there for a few days, accompanying my father on his official trips. Ma always made sure that we ate home-cooked meals. So she would carry a few utensils and a small gas-stove and homemade spices and we would check into the Dak Bungalow or a small, cosy hotel near Jewel Chowk in Jammu city.

When I was much younger, I had accompanied Father on one such trip. It proved to be difficult for him since I refused to eat anything from the hotel. Ultimately, he took me to the Jammu railway station. We stood on the platform while he cracked open peanuts from a packet he had bought, and fed me. As we watched, a train chugged into the station and I was very excited. After the train left, we stood there for a long time,

Father and son, like two philosophers ruminating on life and its meaning. Afterwards, we went for a night show of an Amitabh Bachchan-starrer, *Ram Balram*, and I embarrassed him by eating popcorn from the person sitting next to me. Later, Father also bought me a cricket bat inscribed with Kapil Dev's signature.

And now, we were leaving for good. Everything had changed and the journey was a torment. We reached the Jawahar tunnel, and I looked at Ma. She was mumbling a prayer.

Soon after crossing the tunnel, we reached Ramban, a quaint midway point on the Jammu–Srinagar highway. What we saw there left us stunned. I remember the traffic had been halted due to a minor landslide that was in the process of being cleared. In truck after truck, there were Pandit families escaping to Jammu. In the villages of south and north Kashmir, the situation was far worse than what we had experienced.

Women had been herded like cattle into the backs of trucks. Father and I got out of the taxi to stretch our legs. In one of the trucks, a woman lifted the tarpaulin sheet covering the back and peered outside. There was nothing peculiar about her except the blankness in her eyes. They were like a void that sucked you in. Years later, I saw a picture of a Jewish prisoner in Auschwitz. When I saw his eyes, my mind was immediately transported to that day, and I was reminded of the look in that woman's eyes.

We finally reached Jammu early that evening. After we had crossed the Jawahar tunnel, Father's worries about finding suitable accommodation had taken over. The Dak Bungalow where we usually stayed would be expensive, since we didn't know how long we were going to stay. Eventually we checked into a small, relatively cheap hotel. Ma immediately set up a kitchen on one side of the room and my sister was sent to fetch a bucket of fresh water. Until a few years ago we had not even heard of overhead tanks. It took us a while to understand that the water that came out of taps in Jammu and elsewhere was not fresh water.

On the first day I filled water in a bucket to take a bath. The first mug that I poured over myself singed me. I was reminded of how we would bathe back home in Srinagar. In the winter, Ma would wake us up before sunrise. In the bathroom there would be water steaming in the traditional copper tank. We would have a bath while she kept a set of fresh clothes on a kangri to warm them. We would then dry ourselves vigorously, wear the clothes warmed on the kangri, and snuggle back under our quilts. In summers, just for fun, I would bathe at the tap in the kitchen garden when Ma was away.

In Jammu, for me the biggest symbol of exodus turned out to be a pair of shoes. Back home, my father once saw me playing football at the polo ground with men twice my age, and he was so impressed that he bought me a pair of studded football shoes from a store called Sunchasers. But those shoes had been left behind. The ones I came to Jammu wearing were falling apart. So, Father had bought me a pair of cheap canvas shoes from Gumat market. I despised those shoes. But I understood his position. He had no money and there was total uncertainty about our future.

Our only concern during our last few days in Srinagar had been to somehow survive, to go somewhere where there would be no slogans, no loudspeakers, no fists and middle fingers raised at us, no hit lists, no Kalashnikovs, no freedom songs. So we were relieved to come out of the other end of the Jawahar tunnel.

Once we were in Jammu, other worries took over. Where were we going to live? Where would the money come from? Was everyone else safe—our friends, relatives? Suddenly, the premise that everything was going to be all right in a few months didn't seem plausible at all—it would take much longer to return. But the thought that we might never return still did not cross our minds.

Living in the hotel beyond a few days was not possible. There were hardly any savings to dip into. Father had put all his money into the house. When we had left, he had been extending our attic. He had ordered the choicest deodar wood, and weeks before the crisis erupted the wood had arrived in planks and had been stored in the attic. The carpenter, Farooq, had been called and he had been shown designs for cupboards, a chest of drawers and a wardrobe.

After spending three days in the hotel, Father began to look around for more suitable accommodation.

In the evenings, we would go to the Geeta Bhawan temple in the heart of old Jammu. It was there that the enormity of our tragedy, of our exile in our own country, struck us. The Bhawan had a large central courtyard. Portions of the building had been taken over by families who had nowhere else to go. Rags or saris or blankets or even bed sheets had been hung up to create small, private spaces.

We would all flock to the Bhawan to find out about the welfare of other families. Neighbours met neighbours, brothers met brothers, colleagues met colleagues, and in that courtyard they took stock of the catastrophe that had befallen them.

'*Trath ha se peye*' was the common refrain those days. Lightning had struck us. Some smoked cigarette after cigarette. Women walked to the storage tank to collect water. Everything looked like a nightmare, including the unreliable water supply. Old women wearing their traditional pherans in that heat cooled themselves with bamboo hand-fans.

It was at the Bhawan that the fate of others became evident to us—stories of what had happened in Anantnag, in Sopore, in Baramulla, in Budgam, in Kupwara. In Handwara, a massive crowd had spilled out on the streets on January 25 and the people carried axes and knives and iron rods. Some of them wore shrouds. The procession was in response to an announcement that had been made the night before: 'We have achieved Azadi and tomorrow we will all come out and celebrate in the main market square.' The crowd passed through Pandit localities. 'Take out your Kalashnikovs, let's finish them!' shouted one. At Safa Kadal, the fleeing Pandit families were showered with coins and *shireen* to tell them they were already dead. The mob had shouted: *Ram naam sat hai, akh akis patte hai* (Ram's name is truth, Pandits are leaving one after another). At Poershiyaar, an elderly Pandit saw a young man being brought to the steps leading to the Jhelum. He was being held by his hands and feet. His head was repeatedly banged on a stone step till blood flowed from his nose and mouth.

Those who escaped were on the streets now. We had lost everything—home, hearth, and all our worldly possessions, which had taken generations to build. Everyone mourned over the loss of this or that. An elderly woman known to my mother sat on the steps leading to a small temple, shedding silent tears. Her great-grandmother had passed on some pashmina and shahtoosh shawls to her. She had kept them safe for decades, mothballed for protection, to pass on to the next generation— divided equally between her daughter and her prospective daughter-in-law when the time came. And now they were all lost, left behind in the wilderness of Baramulla.

'I wish I could call my neighbour and request her to keep them safe,' she said.

'Don't be silly,' her husband snapped. 'Don't you realize what your friend has done to us?' He turned to my father and told him what had happened. They were planning to take their possessions with them to Jammu. The man had spoken to a transport company and they had promised to send a mini load-carrier. As they waited a few men arrived, banging at their door. Then they kicked the door in.

They entered menacingly as the old couple cowered in a corner. 'Pandit, I believe you want to leave. *Balaay Dafaa!* Good riddance! Leave, but you cannot take anything with you.' So the mini load-carrier was of no use. The family came to Jammu empty-handed, thankful that they had been allowed to leave unharmed. The old man said, 'I'm sure the neighbours knew. By now they would have taken all your shawls.'

The woman looked crestfallen, and I think her husband immediately regretted what he had said to her with such certainity. Sometimes it is best to leave things ambiguous, suspended, so that some hope remains. I think it was on those steps that the woman lost her will to live.

A few months later, she died in a one-room dwelling.

It was at Geeta Bhawan that I had an experience that could have altered my life forever. One evening I saw some boys and a few elderly men gathering at a ground behind the Bhawan. They wore khaki knickers, and one of them erected a wooden pole in the middle of the ground with a saffron flag on it. Then they formed two rows and put their hands over their hearts and chanted some mantras. One of the men spotted me watching them and signalled me to come towards him.

'Are you a Pandit *sharnaarthi*?' he asked.

He made me sit next to him. Another boy joined us, sitting in front of us on his haunches, listening intently to the man.

'You've been evicted out of your own homes by Muslims. You know that, right?' he asked.

'Yes, they evicted us,' I replied.

'What does it do to you?' he asked.

I was not sure what he meant so I kept looking at him. The boy intervened. 'What Guruji means to ask is whether you feel something inside about it. What do you feel?'

I tried to gauge how I felt about it. For a few seconds, so many images crossed my mind. Of those boys claiming our house. Of the fear on the dark night of January 19. Of the searing heat in my room. Suddenly I felt very hot under the collar.

'I am very angry,' I said.

He looked at me sternly. 'How angry?'

'Very angry.'

'Say it loud. How angry?'

'Very angryyyyyyyyyy!'

'Good,' he said. 'Now the question is: what do you want to do about it? Will you accept it silently like a *napunsak* or do you want to take some action?' he asked.

Napunsak. Impotent. Suddenly I wanted to do something. Suddenly I wanted a gun in my hand and I wanted to kill. I wanted a bomb in my hand and I wanted to throw it in Lal Chowk at one of the processions.

'We are from the RSS. The Rashtriya Swayamsevak Sangh. We will give direction to your anger,' he said. 'Come, let's go join the others,' he continued, looking at the other men.

We went and stood in front of the saffron flag.

'Put your hand on your chest,' the man said.

I had seen them doing this earlier. So I did it exactly as they did. And he made me recite a mantra.

'Come here every day,' he said. 'We meet here every day. We will teach you many things and make a man out of you. A man who is willing to fight for his rights, not only for himself but for his entire community. We are Hindus after all. Have you heard of Parshuram?' he asked.

I had. I knew some of the verses of a poem about the warrior ascetic's dialogue with Lord Ram's younger brother Laxman. I recited some of them. He looked at me, not understanding what I had recited. He did not know those verses. I explained what I had recited.

'Oh, of course, now I remember,' he said, breaking into a smile.

'Come tomorrow, I will see you here,' he said.

They all shook hands with me.

I was so excited I ran all the way from the ground towards the main building of Geeta Bhawan to look for my father. It was very crowded so it took me some time to find him.

'There you are,' Father said the moment he spotted me.

'*Kot osuk gaeb gomut?*' he asked. Where had you disappeared? That was my father's favourite phrase when he was mildly angry. I ingored it and began animatedly telling him about my encounter. I was so excited that I did not see his expression change.

'I am going to see them tomorrow and every day now,' I went on. 'They will teach me how to fight the Muslims who made us flee from our home.'

'Listen, you fool!' My father tried suppressing his anger, but the tone of his voice hit me like a slap. 'We are not here to fight but to make sure that you go to school and get your education.

You don't need to worry about anything else. Where we live, what we eat, where the money will come from—none of it is your concern. You just concentrate on your studies. And, yes, tomorrow we are admitting you into a school.

'And don't you dare meet those men ever again,' he hissed.

Years later, I saw Father reading a report on the slain Ehsan Jafri, brutally done to death by a Hindu mob in Ahmedabad's Gulbarg Society, a predominantly Muslim neighbourhood. As I sat next to him, I read how Jafri had nurtured a nest of barn swallows in his room and to protect them, he would not even switch on the ceiling fan. That day I realized that Father had gifted me something invaluable. Something that enabled me to calmly face an uproariously drunk army general one night in a television news studio. We were there to debate human rights violations in Kashmir and I pointed out that there needs to be zero tolerance towards such crimes. 'How can you say that?' he barked. 'It is they who have forced you out of your homes, turning you into refugees.'

I looked him in the eye and said: 'General, I've lost my home, not my humanity.'

Father's search for suitable accommodation continued. Many Pandit families had rented out rooms from the local people in Jammu. But even that was scary. We had heard many stories of exploitation and harassment by landlords.

After a few days of searching, father finally announced that he had found a place. It was a cheap dharamshala owned by the Rajput community in the middle of a bazaar in the old city. Known as the Rajput Sabha, it had a few rooms reserved for the community members who visited the city, mostly to pay obeisance at the Vaishno Devi shrine. It was also used as a community hall to solemnize marriages and other functions. It was surrounded by shops selling bridal wear. There was a famous sweet shop nearby, and a number of shops where girls arrived in hordes to have their dupattas dyed. The room itself was quite small, and from the ceiling hung a rickety fan, donated by someone in memory of his grandmother.

Unlike the hotel, there were no beds and mattresses here. Apart from a blanket and a bed sheet, we had nothing. For days we slept on newspaper sheets spread on the floor. On a small kerosene stove, Ma cooked and we ate hoping that the power wouldn't go off, leaving us drenched in sweat. It was so hot we couldn't sleep at night. After a week or so, Father bought a couple of cotton mattresses for us to sleep on. The water supply came only once every morning, for about an hour.

On Sundays, I would sneak out to watch the TV series *Mahabharat* while standing on the stairs of a local shopkeeper's house. He would allow his workers to watch it from there, and I would stand quietly with them. At least there was power in Jammu. In Srinagar, they would deliberately cut off electricity at the telecast time of *Ramayan*, and then later *Mahabharat*.

There was another serial that would be telecast right afterwards. It was about a child prodigy called Lekhu who used science to make small changes in the lives of the people of his village. But after *Mahabharat*, all the workers would leave and the shopkeeper's family would bolt the main door. I would then sit on a small bench outside a nearby temple and imagine what Lekhu would have made that day. Father had once told me how one could make a radio with a magnet and a copper wire. Sitting on that bench, I would rack my brains to figure out how I could build a television so I could watch Lekhu's adventures.

It was here at the Rajput Sabha that a deadly psychological blow was inflicted upon Mother. One evening, the compound had been booked by a family for their daughter's marriage. As darkness fell, it was filled with men, women, and children wearing shiny new clothes. The stereo played popular filmy numbers and many danced to the tunes. Late in the night, there was a knock at our door. Mother opened it and found a man standing there with a plate in his hands. 'I was told that *sharnaarthis*—refugees—live here. So I came to offer food.' Before Mother could react, the man put the plate in her hands and turned away. Mother lifted the newspaper sheet covering it. On the plate were rice, dal, and pumpkin curry. Mother stared at it for some time and then she began to weep inconsolably.

The next morning, I accompanied her to the market to buy milk. While standing in the queue, I watched as she initiated a conversation with a woman standing in front of her. 'You know,' she said, 'our home in Kashmir had twenty-two rooms.'

One day our stay at the Rajput Sabha came to an abrupt end. The caretaker had been making noises about the rules of the community centre—nobody was allowed to stay beyond a week or, at the most, a couple of weeks. And we had already been there for more than a month.

Whenever he mentioned the rules, Ma would cook something nice and send it across to the caretaker. And now almost five weeks had gone by and the matter was no longer in his hands. The management had been monitoring our stay and one day the caretaker came and asked us to vacate the room within twenty-four hours.

Packing our few belongings didn't take much time at all. But where to go was a question that loomed like a dark grey cloud over our existence. Once again, father had to go looking for accommodation.

Late that evening he came back and told us, 'I couldn't find anything. We'll have to shift to another dharamshala.' We packed our stuff into an autorickshaw. A week ago, my grandmother had also joined us. She had left Kashmir earlier along with my uncle's family.

The Vinayak Dharamshala's entrance was old, almost hidden behind the façade of a vegetable shop. The first thing I remember of that green building is the smell of ammonia, coming from the filthy urinal located almost in the middle of the building's compound. Our room had a small window that looked out on to a wall. There was a string cot and there were marks of vermilion all over. The blades of the fan were damaged and it was covered with the dust of years. It was very hot and depressing. Ma sat in one corner of the room, on a newspaper sheet. And she cried. Within an hour of us moving in, the electricity went off. Outside, drunk labourers began to shout expletives at each other, jostling for a space to sleep in the compound outside our room. There were too many mosquitoes. After a while, Grandmother was so tired she fell asleep. Even in her sleep, her hand moved as if she were fanning herself. Father brought some food from the Vaishno Dhaba outside, but we had lost our appetite.

We left the room at the first light of dawn. We looked at each other; we resembled chickenpox patients. We went to my uncle's place; he was staying in a one-room dwelling. Together, my father and uncle went out searching again. We applied lime juice on our mosquito bites. My aunt made us some breakfast, but we couldn't stay there for long, as their landlord also frowned upon tenants receiving guests. So we just sat there praying that we would find a place to stay. Father and Uncle returned that afternoon, their faces flushed and their sweat-soaked shirts stuck to their backs. But I could see that Father was relieved. A man called Madan Lal was the reason for that relief.

Years ago, we had arrived late one night in Jammu City. The dak bungalow had no rooms available, so we went from hotel to hotel in the hope of finding a suitable room. It was then that we met Madan Lal, the manager of the Tawi View Hotel, which lay hidden behind a row of car-repair shops. Madan Lal was a Pandit who had settled in Jammu years ago. As he knew my uncle, who bore a striking resemblence to my father, he recognized us. That rainy night he offered us a room and even organized some food and warm tea for us. He was a tough taskmaster and kept the entire hotel very clean.

And now, years later, it was he who rescued us from the roughest storm of our lives. He was now the manager of Hotel Gulmour. It was by sheer chance that he had spotted my father and uncle. Later he would tell this story a hundred times—how he was about to leave the hotel to visit an ailing relative and had almost missed them.

He rented us a room for one thousand rupees, later bringing it down to nine hundred. We shifted immediately. Our room was on the top floor and its windows overlooked a hillock, on which was built a colony. The first thing we saw there was a huge, bright white wall that almost blinded one in the afternoon summer sun. In the coming days, it became a sort of barometer to guage how hot it was on any particular day.

And so began a new chapter in our life. It was the height of summer by then. At the crack of dawn, we had to fetch drinking water from a tap in the basement. So, every morning we spent an hour ferrying water up to our room. It was an arduous task, especially because it was only in the morning that the air cooled down a bit and one could get some sleep. But if one slept in, there would be no water. Nonetheless, ours was still better than the life of those who lived in the refugee camps or in one-room settlements like my uncle's.

The nights were dreadful. After midnight, all the heat absorbed by the city would burst forth, like a dragon from its labyrinth. We would wet Ma's dupattas and drape them over ourselves. By the time we finally drifted off to sleep, it was time to get up again to fetch water. Right after that, it was time to leave for school.

I would wear a red checked shirt and jeans and walk to the main road. When I returned, the sun would be at its zenith. Walking from the main road till the hotel made me dizzy. After every three or four days, I would walk all the way from the school to the hotel—saving the bus fare—and use the saved money to buy a bottle of Gold Spot. Drinking water made me nauseous. I longed for cold water. Sometimes we would get a slab of ice from an exiled family that had a fridge. Later, we made a novel arrangement for cold water. Every morning, I would trundle up to Raghunath Bazaar and buy a slab of ice for a rupee and hurry back with it. We would put it in a polythene bag and place the bag in a small water cooler. That way we managed to get cold water till lunchtime.

That summer we ate very frugally. Most of the time our bellies were filled with water. On many nights I dreamt of our kitchen garden in Srinagar, and that I was having a bath underneath the tap there. 'I wish I had a pipe near my mouth through which I could keep sipping cold water,' my grandmother often said.

We would get a copy of the *Daily Excelsior* every day at the hotel. After he had gone through it, Madan Lal would let me read it. I noticed that far too many obituaries of old people had begun to appear in the newspaper. The harsh summer and the agony of homelessness were taking a heavy toll.

One morning in June 1990, I was sitting in the hotel's reception when I froze at the sight of the front page of the newspaper. It read—'Dreaded militant Latif Lone killed in an encounter'. I wanted to rush up to our room and tell my father about it. But I stayed put and read the whole report. Latif had been shot dead in an encounter with security forces. The report said he had been the mastermind of many ambushes against security forces, including the one outside my house in which two BSF soldiers had been killed. It said that he had received training from the Mujahideen in Afghanistan.

I went upstairs and told my parents. Ma began to cry. She kept saying: *Latifa, jawan-e-rael; Latifa jawan-e-rael.* Latif, he was in the prime of youth; Latif, he was in the prime of youth.

That day, no food was cooked in our room. Ma did not eat even a morsel of food. We couldn't believe that Latif was no more.

We learnt the details of the episode later from Ravi. While every Pandit household in our locality had fled, two had decided to stay back. Ravi's family was one of them. Ravi had recently got a lecturer's job in a government college. He thought nobody would hurt his family. He trusted his friends and colleagues.

On the day Latif was killed, the results of the Class 12 Board Examination had been declared, and he had stood outside Bombay Beauties, holding a Gazette in his hands. He wore a new pathani suit and, like always, his eyes were adorned with kohl. Suddenly, an army gypsy screeched to a halt in front of him, and Latif took to his heels. Behind Bombay Beauties was a barbed-wire fence beyond which were a few houses and open fields. As he was crossing the fence, Latif's salwar got entangled in the wire. The soldiers caught up with him and fired. Latif's aunt, who was standing nearby, tried to come in between, but she could not match the speed of the bullets. He died dangling between the wires. His body was taken away immediately.

Ravi said that at least a hundred thousand people attended his funeral. A few weeks later, one of our erstwhile Muslim neighbours was found hanging from a tree, a few miles from his house. The man was a tailor who sometimes sold cinema tickets in black. He was also an opium addict. Latif's organization had suspected him of passing on information about Latif to the army, so he was abducted, shot in the knees and hung by his neck.

As I read and reread the news report on Latif's death, I remembered one time when Latif had just climbed down after fitting the antenna on Ravi's roof. At the base of the antenna, on a block of wood, I had seen a strange formation and it had fascinated me.

When he came down, I had asked Latif, 'Bhaijaan, what is this?'

He had looked at it, run his hand through my hair as he always did and said, 'Algae!'

PART THREE

From March 1990 onwards, the killings of Pandits in the Valley increased manifold. The news reports coming in from Kashmir were tragic. In the name of Azadi, the Pandits were hounded on the streets and killed brutally. Killings of the Hindu minority had turned into an orgy; a kind of bloodlust. By April, 1990, the mask was completely off. It was not only the armed terrorist who took pride in such killings—the common man on the streets participated in some of these heinous murders as well.

In downtown Srinagar's Chota Bazaar area, thirty-six-year-old telecommunications officer B.K. Ganju had been warned that his name was on a 'hit list' in a neighbourhood mosque. It was March 1990. Fearing for their lives, Ganju and his wife had decided to leave Srinagar the next morning. Early the next morning, their telephone began to ring incessantly. But they did not answer it.

Soon afterwards, there was a loud knock at the door. Mrs Ganju asked who it was.

'Where is Ganju? We have some urgent work with him,' said the voice from outside.

'He has already left for work,' she told them. The calling out and knocking on the door persisted, but she wouldn't open it.

Suddenly, there was silence, and Mrs Ganju went to a first-floor window to look outside. There was nobody at the door. Then she heard noises from one of the rooms below. The strangers were now trying to break in through a window. She urged her husband to hide in the attic, in a drum partially filled with rice.

By that time, the two men had entered the house. One of them was carrying a rifle and the other a pistol. Pushing Mrs Ganju aside, they searched all the rooms and, unable to find her husband, they left.

In old Srinagar, houses are built quite close to each other. One of the Muslim women in Ganju's neighbourhood had seen him hiding in the drum. As the men came out, she signalled to them, telling them what she had seen. The men returned and went directly to the attic and shot B.K. Ganju dead inside that drum.

As they were coming down, Mrs Ganju asked them to kill her as well.

'No, someone should be left to wail over his dead body,' they replied.

In Anantnag, in south Kashmir, the relatives of the renowned Kashmiri poet and scholar Sarvanand Kaul 'Premi' had been urging him to leave the Valley. But Premi had been confident that nobody would touch him. He had spent his whole life with his Muslim neighbours, he said. They will protect me, he told his relatives.

When he was seventeen, Premi had participated in the Quit India movement against British rule. Later, he also played a pivotal role in the Quit Kashmir movement against the Dogra Maharaja of Kashmir, in 1946–47. A brilliant scholar, Premi had translated Tagore's *Gitanjali,* and the Bhagwad Gita into Kashmiri. He was secular to the core—in his prayer room, he kept a rare manuscript of the Koran. After his retirement, he had taught for free for three months a year in two schools, one run by an Islamic and the other a Hindu educational society.

On the night of April 29, 1990, three armed men barged into Premi's house. They ordered the family to assemble in one room. 'Bring all your valuables here,' one of them told a family member. These were brought—jewellery, cash, heirloom pashmina shawls. Then the men ordered all the women to hand over whatever ornaments they were wearing. This was complied with as well. The valuables were packed into a big suitcase which Premi was ordered to carry.

'Where are you taking him?' the women begged of the three men.

'Don't worry, he will return soon,' one of the men said.

As Premi lifted the suitcase, his hand was trembling. After all, he was sixty-six years old. Unable to watch his father struggling, Virender, his twenty-seven-year-old son, insisted on accompanying him.

In the darkness of night, father and son were led away by the armed men. Their family members waited for them all night. But the two did not return.

The police found their bodies hanging from a tree a day later. The men had hammered nails between their eyebrows, where the tilak is applied. Their limbs were broken and their bodies ravaged with cigarette burns. They had been shot as well.

In Bandipora, in north Kashmir, twenty-eight-year-old Girja Tiku worked as a laboratory assistant in a school. Her family had already migrated to Jammu. But, being poor, the family depended heavily on Girja's salary.

So Girja would return to Bandipora every month, from Jammu, to collect her salary. By April, the situation had turned explosive. Her cousin, with whom she was staying in Bandipora's Tikr village, asked her to collect her salary and leave immediately. 'Don't return this time,' he advised her. But she needed the money badly and returned in May again. By then, her cousin had migrated to Jammu, so Girja stayed with a Muslim family—

the head of the house was a friend of Girja's father. The morning after she arrived, she was picked up by four men. Her body was found days later by the roadside.

Years later, a senior commander of the terrorist outfit Hizbul Mujahideen shared Girja Tiku's story with a Bandipora resident. The two had been discussing the early days of militancy in the Valley, and the conversation veered towards the Pandits, and then to the Tiku family. Girja, he said, had been abducted and immediately blindfolded. Four men had taken turns to rape her in a moving taxi. As they were conversing with each other, Girja recognized the voice of one of the men who went by the name Aziz.

'*Aziza, chhetey chukha?* Aziz, are you here as well?' she asked.

Aziz got worried. He knew that Girja had recognized him. So, in a final act of barbarism, they took her to a wood-processing unit and cut her alive on a mechanical saw.

This is what the seekers of freedom were doing to the religious minority.

In June, 1990, Ashwani Kumar, a chartered accountant, was shot at by militants and injured severely. His father went to the police station to request a vehicle to take his son to the hospital. 'Wait for India's helicopter,' the station in-charge told him. When he was finally taken to the main hospital, the doctors refused to treat him. His family managed to somehow shift him to the Soura medical institute, but no doctor touched him there either. He died there.

Many such cases were reported where doctors refused treatment to injured Pandits targeted by militants.

Every time Ma heard such reports, she cried. Every evening, before dinner, she would sit next to Father as he listened to the news bulletin on Radio Kashmir. The news of the killings made her worry about her brother's family, especially Ravi.

'I don't know what is wrong with them, why won't they leave like everybody else,' she often said.

At times, the name of our neighbourhood would be mentioned in the news—an encounter between militants and security forces, or a hand grenade attack, or the army's blasting a building with dynamite to kill militants holed up inside. This made Mother's heart sink and at times like these she would pray.

A few years prior to the exodus, Ravi had fallen off his motorcycle outside the Palladium cinema, and had sustained a deep gash on his knee. The wound was treated in the hospital and Ravi was soon discharged. However, after a few days, when Ravi tried to change the dressing, he could not. The blood had dried up and the bandage was stuck to the wound. Even if touched gently there, Ravi would writhe in pain. He would not let even Ram Joo, the compounder, touch the dressing. He finally came to our house and asked Ma to change it.

Mother took out a fresh roll of bandage, cotton, and antiseptic lotion. She looked Ravi in the eye as she held one corner of his dressing. 'So, what is the maximum speed your motorcycle can reach?' she asked. Ravi's attention was diverted. He opened his mouth to answer Ma's question, but instead let out a loud cry. With one tug, Ma had taken off the dressing. I never understood from where Ma got her courage at times like these.

And now, Ravi and his family were in Srinagar, and we were in Jammu. The concern for their safety robbed Ma of sleep—whatever little she could manage in that heat and amidst the worry of what the morning might bring.

Whenever he could, Ravi visited us in Jammu. On the days he was expected, Ma's entire demeanour would change. She would sing to herself and repeatedly send me to the market to buy things Ravi liked.

'Go and get Cinthol soap; he likes it.'

'Can we ask Madan Lal to keep a few bottles of Thums Up in his fridge?'

'Can you get a packet of Green Label tea? He only drinks that.'

When Ravi would finally appear at our doorstep, tears of joy would run down Ma's cheeks and she would hold him in a tight embrace. Then, for several days, she would stuff him with food.

'Don't apply ghee on my roti,' Ravi would insist.

But his pleas were lost on Ma. She never paid heed. When Ravi protested too much, she would say, 'Two rounds of your college field and this will all disappear.' Then she would turn silent, remembering where Ravi's college was.

'For God's sake, why don't you shift here? Everyone is here, everybody's family is here,' she would then say. Ravi would just laugh, hold her, and say, 'Go and make dum aloo for me.' Ravi had a strong faith in his friendships, thanks to which he didn't feel the need to leave home. After he returned to Srinagar, Ma would go back to her routine of listening to the evening news on the radio.

One day, towards the end of August 1990, we had to vacate the hotel. Madan Lal had been dismissed from service on charges of embezzlement. After he left, the owners spoke about refurbishing the hotel. We knew we had no choice but to find shelter elsewhere.

Near Gumat Chowk there was a chemist's shop from where Father would buy medicines. Over the months, he had come to know the chemist, and as the threat of another move loomed large, Father asked him if he knew of any suitable accommodation. The chemist said his sister lived in a colony near the canal. She was married to an army officer and they had a room to spare. It would cost us five hundred rupees.

That was less than what we were paying at the hotel, so father readily agreed, although we were unsure of what sort of landlords the house owners would turn out to be.

So, with a prayer on our lips, we packed our bags on the first day of September 1990, and shifted to Bhagwati Nagar. The colony was a small, built along a channel of the canal. At the cross section of one of the inner lanes stood a house and we were given a room in the front. Our room was bigger than the one we occupied in the hotel. Ma as usual set up her kitchen immediately in one corner. The chemist's sister lived at the back of the house with her mother-in-law, and both of them were very kind. The old lady of the house even gave us some old durries to put underneath our mattresses. The officer was always away, on duty.

The room wasn't a dark hole and it wasn't damp, but space-wise, it was just one small room. One corner was taken up by the kitchen, and on a long, rickety wooden bench provided by the landlady, Mother set up utensils and other articles.

Every day, Ma got up at the crack of dawn, fearing that she might miss the water supply. It came every morning for precisely one hour, and sometimes less. At dawn, I would sometimes wake up to find Ma sitting with her back against the wall, waiting for the water supply to start. For her, there was nothing as important as making sure that we stored sufficient water every day.

It was in this room that we gradually picked up the pieces of our lives, and began to prepare ourselves for the long haul. It was here that a sense of permanency about our situation set in.

One afternoon when I returned from school, I saw that Father had bought a big desert cooler. A few months later, he managed to save some money and we bought a fridge. That year we were without a television, though. It was the following year that Father bought one, on instalments, similar to the BPL television set we'd had back home.

I left the room early in the morning for school. I hated the dull, monotonous, factory-like rhythm of our lives. Each morning everyone had to contribute to the water-collecting labour. We had to fetch bucket after bucket of water and also bathe, all within an hour. Also, we had to share the water supply with the owners and another tenant family. Sometimes, the water supply would play truant for days. So the men would go to a neighbouring vacant plot and bathe under an open tap there. I found this very embarrassing since passers-by on the street could see me. But it was better than not taking a bath at all. During such moments, I always remembered home. My parents often spoke about a village where they had been posted soon after their marriage, where one could just dig the earth with one's hands to make water appear.

Around this time, all the refugees who had fled from Kashmir had been asked to register their names, and each family was provided with a ration card. It was like a document of citizenship, identifying one as a 'migrant' and enabling government employees to collect salaries, or a cash relief of five hundred rupees in the case of the non-salaried families. For families like ours it was a hard life, but we managed somehow. But for non-salaried families, sustenance was tough. It was just not possible to support a family on the meagre stipend of five hundred rupees doled out by the government, and the small monthly ration of rice and sugar.

Every ration card had to include a photograph of the male head of the family, along with his wife. So in some cases, husbands and wives made separate ration cards to ensure that more money came in. To do this, many got their pictures taken with migrant labourers from Bihar and elsewhere. It was shameful, but there was little else one could do in those treacherous times. In Kashmir, we learnt, they had made fun of this misery as well by creating yet another ditty: *Ram naam sat hai, Paanc'hh hath te batte hai* (Ram's name is truth, it's five hundred rupees and rice [for the Pandits]).

In Jammu, over the past few months, things had been taking an ugly turn. Initially, like us, the Jammuites thought our exodus was temporary. Though they benefitted economically because of us, they developed an antipathy towards us. For them, we were outsiders. Within months, invectives had been invented for us. The most popular among them was:

Haath mein Kangri munh mein chholey
Kahan se aayey Kashmiri loley

Kangri in hands, chickpeas in their mouth
From where did these Kashmiri flaccid penises come?

When Father heard this for the first time, he did not quite understand the insult. All he said was, 'But we hardly eat chholey!'

This was mainstream India for us. Our own Hindu brothers and sisters who took out a procession every Basant Panchami to safeguard Hindu rights were turning into our oppressors as well.

The most tyrannical were the landlords. Barring a few thousand unfortunate people who lived in miserable conditions in the refugee camps, most of us were forced to rent rooms from the local residents. Many locals wanted the extra money they could earn by renting out rooms. So often, people built additional rooms quickly—hencoop like—to rent them out. But once a family started living there, the landlords tried to control every aspect of their lives—how much water they were allowed to use, how much television they could watch, how many guests could visit, what they could cook or not cook. In many houses, the owners would hover around the tenant family's room and keep a tab on the number of shoes outside. Our language, our pronunciation became an object of ridicule. Just like it did in Kashmir during that crackdown in the early 2000s, when the poor Kashmiri faced ridicule on account of his limited Hindi.

There is one particular incident that I can never forget. One of our relatives had a young son, hardly twelve years old. While going for a school picnic, the boy felt like buying a packet of potato chips and a soft drink to supplement the food his mother had cooked for him. He had no money, so he borrowed twenty rupees from a ruffian on his street, promising to return the money along with an interest of ten rupees. But days later, he was unable to repay the money. Out of fear, he never shared his predicament with his family. The ruffian kept threatening him.

One day, the boy stepped out of his house to play with his friends when the ruffian caught hold of him. He was carrying a screwdriver with which he stabbed the boy in the abdomen. The boy tried to run away and even begged a shopkeeper for help. But nobody came forward to help him. He died on the steps of the shop he had bought the packet of chips and soft drink from.

His parents were shattered. His mother was inconsolable. When he had stepped out of his house for the last time, the boy had snatched a piece of cucumber his mother had been eating. That memory remained and was now cutting his mother's heart like a thorn.

The Jammu of the early nineties was in the grip of criminal elements. Each area had its don, and some of them had links with arms and drug smugglers. Every day, the newspapers would report a stabbing or a shootout. Some unruly elements thought that since the Pandit community was in distress, their girls would be freely available for exploitation. Out of sheer desperation, and to escape the hell of their daily lives, a few girls made that compromise. They eloped with young men who promised them a better life. But in most cases, such offers to elope were resisted. After all, we had escaped from the Valley to protect our lives, and more than our lives, our dignity.

Since it was a relatively new colony, Bhagwati Nagar had limited transport facilities. A Matador minibus would come every half hour or so and it was much coveted. Since I would leave for school early in the morning, I would catch it daily, sitting on the 'friend' seat, next to the driver's.

After a few weeks, I noticed that the driver had begun to behave very sweetly towards me, even letting me ride for free. I thought we had forged a kind of friendship and that was why he made this gesture. But soon, I would be proved wrong. One fine day it became clear what he had wanted all along. He had in fact set his eyes on a Kashmiri girl from our neighbourhood. Her family came from a village in Kashmir and they were trying to retain their dignity in a small rented room. The girl went to my school. The driver had decorated his minibus with stickers carrying mushy messages. On the back, he had put a sticker that had an image of an arrow piercing through a heart, underneath which was written: *Love for sale, 100% discount.*

The driver wanted to convey his love to the girl. He had bought a greeting card for the purpose. Now he wanted me to write a nice mushy message inside the card. *Kavita-type,* he said. Then he put his hand in his shirt pocket and fished out a red sketch pen. 'Here, write with this,' he said. He grinned and I could see his tobacco-stained teeth.

The bait that he would take no fare from me from then onwards proved too tempting. I took the sketch pen from him, and after thinking for a few seconds, I wrote:

> *Mountains can fly, rivers can dry,*
> *You can forget me, but never can I*

'*Ab iska matlab bhi samjha do, praava.*' Now tell me what this means, brother. I told him. His face broke into another grin. He took the card and kept it carefully in the glove box. Of course, when the conductor came, he waved him away.

In the evening, as I was walking back home, I saw that girl's father approaching from the other end of our street. He walked slowly, a wet towel on his head. He looked at me and smiled. 'Namaskar,' I greeted him. '*Orzu, durkoth.*' He wished me well-being and strong knees. 'How is your father?' he asked and without waiting for my reply, he continued, 'You know, the landlord is troubling us too much. Every day he comes and takes oil from us, or sugar, or rice. This would never have been a problem in Shahar. But here, you know what hard times have befallen us.'

'Anyway, I'm just worried about—,' he mentioned his daughter. 'Keep an eye on her, will you?'

The greeting card flashed in front of my eyes. And my writing in red sketch pen. And the mushy poem I had scrawled.

Mountains can fly, rivers can dry,
You can forget me, but never can I

I mumbled something and fled. I reached home, but the image of the girl's father did not leave me. I tried hard to forget about him. I went to the rooftop to look at a girl in the neighbourhood. I tried watching TV. I tried reading *A Tale of Two Cities*. But the image of that man did not leave me. I dreamt of him that night.

The next morning, I woke up, got ready quickly, and picked up my school bag. I walked slowly towards the main road. I stood at one spot, waiting for the Matador to arrive. After a while, I saw the red-and-yellow board of the Matador. The driver stopped right in front of me. That was another privilege extended to me. I got in and sat on the friend seat. He shook hands with me, another privilege.

In the morning he always lit incense and played bhajans by Chanchal. There was also a fresh garland of marigold flowers in front of a deity's picture. The Matador moved forward. I had made up my mind.

'*Praava, O card deeyiein*' I asked him in broken Dogri to hand over the card. His face lit up. He must have thought I had come up with another killer line.

I took the card and opened it up, as if expecting it to be blank inside. But there were the lines, in thick red. 'Here, the pen.' The driver held it in his hand.

And then I did it. While I was at it, and it took me two seconds perhaps, I kept looking at his face. At first he didn't notice, his eyes were on the road. But the sound of the paper tearing made him look at it and he braked abruptly. He let out a barrage of expletives. He hit me hard on the back of my head. I hit him back, just like he had, on the back of his head. I was shaking with anger. I don't know where I got the courage from, but I just got it. Afterwards, I don't remember how many blows landed on my body. My spectacles fell off, but luckily they did not break. I was thrown out of the Matador.

While hitting me, the driver had scratched my face badly. And the back of my head was hurting. But I was smiling. In spite of the pain, I felt very light. There was a buoyancy in my step. Most importantly, the images of the girl's father dissolved. His checkered towel disappeared. His eyes, a film of pain over them, were no longer visible to me. All I could hear was his voice echo in my head—Take care of her, will you?

Yes, I will keep an eye on her. *Mountains can fly, rivers can dry,* but she will always remain a dream for that illiterate driver. I walked fast. The barber had just opened his shop, and he was sweeping last night's hair off the broken floor. I entered, picked up a comb nonchalantly, and ran it through my hair. Then I turned sideways and checked my profile. I looked at my cheap shoes. For months, I had hated them, wishing that their soles would come off so that I could ask Father to buy me another pair. But now, standing at the barber's, I looked at them and at the cheap jeans I wore. They looked so appropriate, so rebellious.

I ran to the baker. He was just throwing his first cooked bread back in the oven as an offering. I bought myself a naan, and sat there at the baker's counter, eating it slowly.

I went to school, but I had lost interest in my studies. I felt stifled at the sight of my classmates' hopping from one class to another, discussing a theorem or some law of Physics. That whole season, I stuck to reading Sarat Chandra Chattopadhyay's *Srikanta*. I sought solace from the story of his travel to

Burma and imagined myself in a ship that had set sail for some distant land. I wanted to fall in love with older women, like Srikanta had.

Forging friendships with some rowdy boys who were at the bottom of the class, I would sit with them at one lonely end of the canal where nobody went and the water gushed out like white foam from a small outlet. Relatives of those who had died would perform religious rites for the deceased there. Often, the coconuts used in such rites would float towards us and we would pick them up and eat them. Through those boys, I also got rare access to the first floor of Raja tea stall, next to my school. It was reserved for the boys who were only into beating up other boys from rival gangs. We would sit there, drinking tea, and taking puffs from a lone Gold Flake cigarette, listening to Kishore Kumar songs.

I had become a rebel. And I was aware of this change in me. In my neighbourhood, I had made some friends. There were the three Suri brothers, who were very kind. I visited their family and without any bitterness, I joked about their 'Dogra' traits, while they made fun of my Kashmiri ways.

One evening, I went to their house. The eldest Suri son had just returned from the old city. 'Don't venture out,' he warned me. He said there was a lot of anger on the streets and Dogra mobs were beating up Pandits in several places. That morning, two Pandit boys had entered the premises of the Ranbir Singh boys high school in the old city. They were carrying a crude bomb that exploded in the hands of one of them. He died instantly, while his accomplice's hand was severed. The accomplice was arrested by the police. The news had spread like wildfire and the locals thought the bomb was meant to kill the schoolboys. So, as the word spread, Pandits were beaten up across the city.

The eldest Suri son said he had seen placards hanging around the necks of dogs that read, 'I am a Kashmiri Pandit'.

It came to be known later that the two boys had intended to target a group of jailed Kashmiri terrorists who had been brought from the prison to write a board exam.

Not everyone had their fathers to guide them if they strayed, as, luckily, I had. There was a lot of anger among the residents of the refugee camps. Most of them were non-salaried families, especially from the villages. Back home, they had owned big houses, and apple and walnut and almond orchards. But now that was all gone. They were solely dependent on government dole.

It was a pathetic existence. Many fell ill with diseases that were hitherto unknown to the community. In the first year alone, many elderly people died of sunstroke, and snake and scorpion bites. Children became infected with fungal diseases, and scabies became rampant in the unhygienic camps. Doctors reported hundreds of cases of stress-induced diabetes. Heart disease and hypertension made their way in our lives. Many fell into depression. There were severe privacy issues as well. Young couples were forced to live in small enclosures with their parents. This first led to an erosion in sexual abilities and then to a reduced birthrate. Medical surveys conducted around that time said that the Kashmiri Pandits in exile had aged by ten to fifteen years. Many in the camp spoke of revenge.

In one camp lived a woman whose young son was killed by his friends in Baramulla. They had taken him to a shop where a few of them caught hold of him while one of them downed the shutter on him. But he was physically very strong and put up a brave fight. He even managed to snatch their only Kalashnikov rifle. But he had no understanding of its functioning and could not unlock it. Meanwhile his assailants overpowered him and one of them fired at him. He was badly injured whereupon they pounced on him, gouged out his eyes and cut out his tongue.

The boy's mother refused to believe that her son was no more. So, every afternoon she would cook food for him and keep it on a parapet outside her tent. I saw her one day while she was cooking food for her dead son. She spoke to a neighbour while she lovingly placed the food on the parapet. 'He won't eat if the rice is not crispy,' I heard her saying.

In 1991, a family from Shopian came to live in the Muthi refugee camp. Pyare Lal Tickoo had been a cloth merchant associated with the local traders' union. The Tickoos lived in Shopian's Batpora locality, home to 112 Pandit families. After the nightmare of January 19, many Pandit families left their homes, fearing for their lives. By April, sixty families had left. By May, another thirty left. Only twelve families, including the Tickoos, decided to stay back.

On June 16, Pyare Lal Tickoo's son, Rajinder, left home for Shopian hospital where he had been training in the accounts department. On his way back home later that afternoon, Rajinder went to a friend's shop near the town's main bus stand. It was here that a group of militants who had been following him from the hospital shot at him. Rajinder was hit by four bullets and he died on the spot.

Someone ran to his house and informed the senior Tickoo about his son's death. The father ran to the bus stand and spotted his son lying alone in a pool of blood. There was a bullet near his corpse. Pyare Lal Tickoo picked it up. It read—Made in China. The body was taken to the hospital where a post-mortem was conducted. Once it was over, Pyare Lal Tickoo carried his son's body in his arms. In the refugee camp, he would recall later—

'When I had my son's body in my arms, I held it close to my heart. I was reminded of Raja Harishchandra's predicament at losing his son.'

There was no priest available for Rajinder's last rites. They cremated him quickly. Nobody among their Muslim neighbours came to offer their condolences.

All the remaining Pandit families of Batpora took refuge in Tickoo's house that night. Late at night, the deputy commissioner of Shopian appeared at their doorstep asking them if they required any security.

'Whatever had to happen has already happened. Now it is up to you to provide us with security or not,' Pyare Lal told him. The officer left in a huff.

No security was provided. Three days later, the Tickoos collected the ashes of their beloved son. Soon after that, all the Pandit families of Batpora left Kashmir for good.

Before leaving, Pyare Lal had tried handing over their two cows to their neighbours. The cows gave five litres of milk in the morning and about seven litres in the evening. But nobody was willing to take them. So, finally, the Tickoo family let them loose. And they left to spend the rest of their lives in exile. A month after they left, all Pandit houses were ransacked by the locals and everything was looted. Then most of the houses were set afire. The remaining houses were destroyed in another fire in 1995. The cloth shop owned by Pyare Lal was looted as well. Later, it was taken over by the government for widening the road.

The Tickoos owned a huge walnut and apple orchard. The walnut orchard produced about two and a half lakh rupees worth of walnuts per season. Many Muslim neighbours approached them later, throughout the nineties, advising them to sell their land. But the Tickoos refused every time.

In 2003, without seeking their consent, the land owned by the Tickoos and other Pandit families was acquired by the state government to construct an Industrial Training Institute. In some cases, revenue records were tampered with by tehsil and revenue officials sympathetic to the majority community.

In his petition to the state revenue department, Tickoo wrote—

'During the past four years . . . the land owned by Pandits is being acquired ostensibly "for public purposes" under a deliberate plan to thwart their chances of return by "finishing [off] their immovable property." In Ward no. 1 of Batpora, the residential land of Pandit families—Lahoris, Sathus, Kitchloos and Panditas, that together measures 35-40 kanals, was taken over for building [a] bus stand. Sadly, Government of India that depends on state authorities for feedback did not try to intervene.'

By the mid 2000s, these episodes become common occurrences. Wherever there is a chance, there are attempts to usurp land or other property belonging to the Pandits. In the early eighties, a prominent Pandit lady, Tarawati, of the village Kolpur near the famous Mansbal Lake, acquired a tract of land for building a temple. A Shivling, vandalized by the tribal invaders in 1947, was established inside. Then in 1990, the Pandit exodus takes place and nobody is left to take care of the temple. In 2006, the Pandit community learns that a fire brigade station is coming up close to the temple and it might have encroached upon the temple land. The Pandits of that village, now living in exile, get together and collect funds to rebuild the temple. They then contact the revenue officials and are told that there is no mention of the presence of a temple in the revenue records.

In September 2012, I meet R.K. Tickoo outside a newspaper office in Srinagar. He has been trying to contact journalists to highlight his plight. Two of his agricultural plots in Wadwan in Budgam district have been illegally occupied by his Muslim tenants. Even after the tehsildar declared it to be an illegal occupation, senior revenue officials are refusing to issue an order in his favour. 'I have been on leave for fifteen days and have been endangering my life, visiting Budgam daily,' he tells me. 'I just need money to be able to send my son for engineering.'

Nine days after Rajinder Tickoo's murder, a group of people entered the house of Brij Lal Kaul in Shopian district's Harman village. Kaul worked as a driver with the Rice Research Station on the Wanpoh–Kulgam road. He had sent his son and daughter to Jammu earlier for their safety. That night, the group caught hold of Kaul and his wife, Chhoti, and pulled them out of their home. They were tied behind a jeep and dragged for three kilometres. But there was still some life left in their mutilated bodies. So they were shot dead.

Later, an acquaintance performed their last rites in the corridor of the house the Kauls had so lovingly built. They were cremated discreetly nearby.

My father continually urged me to study. But it was very difficult. I wanted some private space, and that was impossible. I would sometimes hang a sheet between the television and the string cot to hide myself from the rest of the room. I liked to think that I was in a room of my own. I imagined myself in my first-floor room back home in Srinagar, in the room with the wooden bookshelf.

In exile, salaries of those in government service were being paid. But the employees could not be accommodated in their respective departments in Jammu. So, like everyone else, Father and Ma would visit their office in Jammu once a month, collect their salaries, and return. It seemed like a nice arrangement. But after a few months, unemployment for my father's generation meant that all of them would just sit and think about exile and the difficulties it posed. Some of the younger lot had found work elsewhere, but most people like my parents were at the stage where beginning to work in an entirely different set-up would have been a nightmare. Since they had so much time at their disposal, we would receive a steady stream of guests from early morning till late evening—my parents' colleagues, former neighbours, new neighbours, friends, relatives. This made having a little privacy even more difficult.

With whatever little money I could save, I had bought a few audio cassettes of the music of the popular films of those days. But there was no cassette player to play them on. Our Philips two-in-one had been left behind. Late in the night, while everyone slept, or tried to sleep, I would climb up to the rooftop and listen to songs over a small pocket transistor. I dreamt of saving enough money to buy a Walkman.

Around this time, in 1991, a catastrophe struck our family again. Though we all helped, a large chunk of the housework was left to Ma. She ran the kitchen and tended to all the cleaning, among other chores. The lifting of countless heavy buckets of water had taken a toll on her back. One morning as she bent down to mop the floor, a cry escaped her lips and she fell down. She was in extreme pain and she was unable to get up.

We took her to a doctor immediately; he explained that the alignment of some of her vertebrae had altered, putting pressure on her spinal cord. She was advised complete bed rest. With her completely grounded, the kitchen duty fell to my sister. Father and I pitched in as well, helping her as much as we could. She was in college after all and needed time to study.

It took more than two months for Ma to recover enough to get out of bed. She could walk a little and do light household chores, but she had to wear an orthopedic belt around her waist almost all the time. The doctor also said that she could no longer sit or sleep on the floor. So we had to make a wooden bed for her. But now the problem was that in that small room there was no way we could set up a kitchen for her to stand and work in. We did not want to leave this accommodation, but we were left with no choice. It was a question of Ma's health.

So, we resumed the search once again. This time, Father sought a room with a separate kitchen. Though we knew that we would have to pay more rent, it was a small price to pay for Ma's well-being.

After a week or so, Father found a room with a small kitchen in a house very close by. The house owner was a government employee, and his wife stayed at home. They had four children. The youngest was a boy, so we understood why they had four children.

The day we moved I was quite happy. At least there was a separate kitchen now. Also, along the room, there was a small space, a store of sorts, where I could create my own little space. There were other problems though. The bathroom of the house was without a door. It just had a thin curtain and each time one had to use it, one had to approach and ask—*Koi hai?* If there was someone inside, the person made his presence felt by shouting back *haan* or by coughing a little.

But soon, our stay in that house turned into a nightmare. The owner and his wife were just the sort of landlords we had heard so much about. Every afternoon, the woman sent her children to our room. They would sit there, and even gradually started sleeping there. One day the owner told Father that he wanted my sister to teach his children. 'Just an hour or so, to help with their homework etc.,' he said casually. Father refused, saying his daughter was too busy for that. This did not go down well with them. Then one day, we objected to their children spending too much time in our room. From then on, it all went downhill. The owner started accusing us of spending too much time in the bathroom. 'Every time you go, the water tank is emptied,' he said. That was hardly true. We treated water as if it were a precious jewel.

One of his rules was that no meat should be cooked by us. In exile anyway, we could not afford it. But, we found it tough to adhere to the rule during festivals like Shivratri. Nonetheless, we abided by it strictly. When he could find nothing else, the man accused us of cooking meat in our kitchen. When he left for office, his wife would take over. She spent the whole day on a cot they had placed right outside our room. She had taught her children to shout Kashmiri *loley*. Then they also began raising objections whenever guests stayed overnight, which happened only when Ravi or his parents came to visit us from Kashmir for a day or two.

One day, Ravi's father came to visit, and Ma was very happy. It was the first time her brother had come to visit us after Ma's illness. But when he arrived, the landlady began to create an ugly scene outside our room, accusing us of taking undue advantage of their good nature. Ma tried to reason with her but the landlady went on and on. Uncle understood that it would not be wise for him to stay. So he spent the night at another relative's home. That night, Ma cried. She could not believe that her brother had come to her house and could not stay overnight. What's more, she was unable to even feed him all the food she had spent the day cooking so lovingly.

Then one day they attempted a very dirty trick. One of the cable TV wires ran close to their roof. One of them spliced another wire to it and ran this wire down towards our room window. The cable TV operator, who was very ill-tempered, would pay sudden visits to rooftops to check if anyone had hooked onto his cable without paying. That day he arrived and went straight to the roof of the house. And there he discovered the wire, one end of which touched our window. He came down and thumped his fist on our door. He was shouting expletives. Father tried his best to tell him that we were not responsible for this, but he would not listen. At one point, his abuses became so unbearable that Father gave it back to him. He pushed Father roughly. Luckily, at that point, I returned with one of the Suri brothers and, together, we diffused the situation. But while leaving he threatened us with dire consequences. Father was both angry and aghast. 'You are a dirty man,' he told the owner when he came later. 'We are in exile. I would not even wish such a thing on a demon like you,' he said. The owner tried to shout him down but was left fumbling for a response. In his heart, he knew what he had done.

A week after that ugly episode, we packed our bags again and shifted to yet another house. Seventeen years later, when we were shifting to a house of our own in a Delhi suburb, Father remembered that incident and how quickly we had gotten into the habit of packing our belongings and shifting. 'I could have opened up a packer and mover company,' he quipped. We all smiled. We also counted the number of times we had shifted house since the day we left home.

It roughly came to be around twenty. It may have been even twenty-two times, the same as the number of rooms in our house that Ma talked continually about.

The episode with the landlord affected Ma deeply and triggered another bout of back pain. The orthopaedician who examined her said her condition was beyond any treatment available in Jammu. 'You will have to take her to Ludhiana, or Delhi,' he said.

We were still very unsure of going to Delhi. Ludhiana seemed a more plausible option. The doctor gave us a letter of recommendation for one of his senior colleagues at the Christian Medical College, Ludhiana, and five days later, Ma, accompanied by my father and uncle, took an overnight train to Ludhiana. 'You are the man of the house till I return,' Father said. 'Take care of your sister.'

They returned two days later. Ma had grown thinner and her cheeks were sunken in and I suddenly realized that she had aged a great deal in the last few months. The specialist in Ludhiana had advised that she be administered a series of injections under anaesthesia. Each injection cost a few thousand rupees. Father had carried some cash in anticipation, and Ma had already been given one injection. They were to return for another in a month.

The question was—where would the money for the next injection come from? My uncles offered money, but it was not a question of just one more injection. Over the next few months, many more injections would need to be administered.

It was then that Father thought of the middlemen from Kashmir who had begun to make the rounds of Pandit settlements in Jammu. Some of our erstwhile neighbours had realized that we were in an acute financial crisis and that this was the right time to buy our properties at a fraction of what they were really worth. The houses of Pandits who had lived in posh colonies were much in demand. Many in Kashmir wanted to shift their relatives, who stayed in villages or congested parts of the city, to better houses, to better lives. You would be sitting in your home when a man would suddenly arrive at your doorstep. 'Asalam Walekum,' he would greet you while removing his shoes at your doorstep. Once inside, he would embrace you tightly. He would not come empty-handed. He always carried symbols of our past lives with him—a bunch of lotus stems, or a carton of apples, or a packet of saffron. He sat cross-legged beside you, running his eyes over the room—over the kitchen created by making a boundary of bricks and empty canisters, over the calendar depicting your saints, over your clothes hanging from a peg on the wall, and over to your son, sweating profusely in one corner and studying from a Resnick and Halliday's physics textbook. He would nod sympathetically, accepting a cup of kahwa, and begin his litany of woes. 'You people are lucky,' he would say. 'You live in such poor conditions, but at least you can breathe freely. We have been destroyed by this Azadi brigade, by these imbeciles who Pakistan—may it burn in the worst fires of hell!—gave guns to. We cannot even say anything against them there, because if we do, we will be shot outside our homes. Or somebody will throw a hand grenade at us.' He would then sigh and a silence would descend upon the room, broken only by his slurps.

'Accha, tell me, how is Janki Nath? What is his son doing? Engineering! Oh, Allah bless him!' He would patiently finish his kahwa while you sat wondering what had brought him to your doorstep. It was then that he came to the point.

'Pandit ji,' he would begin. 'You must be wondering why I am here. I remember the good old days when we lived together. Whatever education we have, it is thanks to the scholarship of your community. *Tuhund'ie paezaar mal chhu*—it is nothing but the dirt of your slippers. Anyway . . .' He would pause again.

'I pray to Allah that before I close my eyes, I may see you back in Srinagar. But right now, it is so difficult. Tell me, what is your son doing? Oh, it's his most crucial board exam this year! Pandit ji, do you have enough money to send him to study engineering, like Janki Nath's son? I can see that you don't have it. This is why I am here.'

And then he would ask the crucial question: *Tohi'e ma chhu kharchawun?* Do you wish to spend?

This was a well-thought-of euphemism he had invented to relieve you of the feeling of parting with your home. 'Do you wish to spend?' meant 'Do you want to sell your home?'

'You have had no source of income for months now,' he would continue. 'This is all I can offer you for your house. I know it is worth much more, but these are difficult times even for us.'

If you relented, he would pull out a wad of cash.

'Here, take this advance. Oh no, what are you saying? Receipt? You should have hit me with your shoe instead. No receipt is required. I will come later to get the papers signed.'

He would also forcibly leave a hundred-rupee note in your son's hands and leave. A few days later, a neighbour would come around and ask 'Oh, Jan Mohammed was here as well?'

'His son has become the divisional commander of Hizbul Mujahideen,' the neighbour would inform you.

Most of us did not have a choice. By 1992, the locks of most Pandit houses had been broken. Many houses were burnt down. In Barbarshah in old Srinagar, they say, Nand Lal's house smouldered for six weeks. It was made entirely of deodar wood. The owner of Dr Shivji's X-ray clinic, Kashmir's first, was told his house in Nawab Bazaar took fifteen days to burn down completely. At places where Pandit houses could not be burnt down due to their proximity to Muslim houses, a novel method was employed to damage the house. A few men would slip into a Pandit house and cut down the wooden beam supporting the tin roof. As a result, it would cave in during the next snowfall. Then the tin sheets would be sold and so would the costly wood. Within a few months, the house would be destroyed.

A few weeks after my parents' trip to Ludhiana, my uncle came to our room, accompanied by a middleman. 'He is offering to buy our house,' Uncle said.

He put a number in front of us. 'This is ridiculously low,' Father said. 'This is much less than what I have spent on it in the last few years alone.'

'I know,' the man said. 'But you have no idea what has become of your house. After you left, miscreants ransacked it completely. They took away even your sanitary fittings and water ran through your house for months. A few walls have already collapsed. It is in a very poor state now.'

Nobody said a word. From her bed, Ma finally spoke.

'How does it look from outside?'

'The plaster has broken off completely, but your evergreens are growing well. They are touching your first-floor balcony now.'

And so, home is lost to us permanently. Ma is taken to Ludhiana and the injections are administered. It takes her months to recover.

Sometime ago, in September 2012, I meet an old Pandit scholar in Srinagar who never left Kashmir. He was abducted by militants three times but always returned unscathed. We are in his study where he sits surrounded by books. On the wall on the left are pictures of Swami Vivekananda, Swami Vididhar—a revered saint of Kashmir—and Albert Einstein. He tells me about an incident that occurred in 1995. He was cycling back home from a temple when he was stopped by a Muslim professor he knew. 'What are you doing here? Go to Bae'bdaem, some very rare books stolen from Pandit houses have been put on sale there,' he told him. The scholar cycled furiously to Bae'bdaem and found that in a shed, a boatman had put thousands of books and rare manuscripts on sale for twenty rupees per kilo. The shed swarmed with foreign scholars from Europe. The boatman spotted him. 'You look like a Pandit, are you?' he asked. 'Then your rate is different; it is thirty rupees.'

The scholar placed a hundred-rupee note in the boatman's hand. 'I will give you a hundred rupees for each book and this is the advance,' he told him. The scholar picked up whatever he could, including a fifteenth-century Sanskrit commentary on the verses of Lal Ded and Maheswarnanda's *Maharathamanjari*.

But in exile, scholarship is lost. Young boys and girls work hard in the refugee camp schools and diligently prepare for their board exams while their parents make bank demand drafts to pay for engineering entrance exams. Everybody wants to go to a good college in Maharashtra, or Karnataka, and escape the wretchedness of exile. Everybody wants to earn money and rebuild their lives. But there is no learning now. No one among us would be nicknamed Sartre now.

I wanted to run away as well, but not to Maharashtra or Karnataka. I wanted to escape the drudgery of boring classroom lectures. The results for the higher secondary exams were declared and I had performed averagely as usual. I think Father was embarrassed by my results. I offered him no passage to a secure future. He was unsure about what I would do. But I think by that time I had some clue. I was determined to do something different; I was determined to defy. When I closed my eyes, I imagined a bright round mass of white light inside my chest.

I followed that light one day and arrived in Chandigarh. Though Father initially opposed it, I had decided to join a college there. That was how I escaped Jammu. In Chandigarh I felt no pressure to work hard at my studies. Instead, I forged friendships with people older than me. They were comrades who read Gorky and Dostoevsky, and Nietzsche and Camus, and Chekhov and Flaubert. With them, I also read Weston La Barre's *The Ghost Dance*. I spent days at the State Library, reading writers they would talk of. At night, over egg paranthas and tea at Ranjan's shack outside the General Hospital, they recited the poetry of Avtaar Singh Paash and Shiv Kumar Batalvi. I visited Talwindi Salem, where Paash had lived and where he was killed by Sikh extremists some years ago. In his house, I saw the table on which he had scribbled: *Know what how why*. That round mass of white light inside my chest turned brighter.

I was in college when I received a letter from my sister in Jammu. 'Madan Lal Uncle has passed away,' she informed me. He lived in a small room near ours. When I visited my parents during my college holidays, he would come over and shake hands with me. 'You are a man now,' he would say, while Ma went to the kitchen to prepare a cup of kahwa for him. Sometimes he would come by in the evening and slip a few roasted cashewnuts into my hand. In his last days, he had lost his mind, my sister wrote. He would go up to the terrace of his house and shout all night from there. Father and others took him to the hospital where he died a few days later. He died homeless, away from his land, away from the benevolent gaze of his forefathers.

The next letter I received from home carried good news. Ravi's family had finally decided to shift to Jammu. Both Ravi and his sister had reached marriageable ages. Ravi was hoping that he would be transfered to Jammu since no Kashmiri Pandit family was willing to send their daughter to Srinagar.

At the Bagh-e-Bahu garden, Ravi finally met Asha—the girl who would be his bride. She was very talented, a gold-medalist, Ravi said, in Zoology. 'Together,' I quipped, 'you two complete the life sciences.'

Soon after their engagement, without telling Ravi, I went to see Asha, who taught at my former school. I told her who I was and she took me to her lab, where, surrounded by animal specimens preserved in formaldehyde, she brought me a bun-omelet and a soft drink. 'Which one will you have?' she asked. 'Thums Up,' I replied. She smiled. 'Like him,' she whispered. I was so happy, I had butterflies in my stomach. A few weeks later, Ravi received his transfer to Gool, a small town in the Udhampur division. Some areas around Gool were affected by militancy, but Gool itself was peaceful, Ravi told us.

In the autumn of 1993, Ravi and Asha were married. All the affairs of the marriage were handled by Ravi's friend Irshad. He stayed until every ritual was solemnized; until every feast was partaken of. In between the festivities, the two friends would sit in a corner and exchange whispers and quiet laughter—of the heady days at Kashmir University. A girl's name—Sushma—would come up often. Ravi had once been in love with her.

There are pictures of those days—of Ravi and Asha picnicking at the Bagh-e-Bahu; of them at Patnitop, a tourist resort. They came to visit me in Chandigarh and we watched a movie and then ate at Hot Millions restaurant. A year later, Shubham was born. I sent them a greeting card from Chandigarh and two weeks later, I boarded a night bus to Jammu to hold my nephew in my arms. Asha and I corresponded and some of these letters reflected what I had been reading in the last two years. *'Ye kus se gav Camus*—Who is this Camus?' Ravi would enquire teasingly and I would hesitantly break into a long speech.

Those years passed like a Mobius strip.

I returned to Jammu after my final year exams. A few months later the results were declared and I had scored the same—average marks. But in my heart I carried the best education, of Paash's immortal lines—

Sabse khatarnaaq hota hai/murda shaanti se bhar jaana
Na hona tadap ka/ sab kucch sehan kar jaana
Ghar se nikalna kaam par/ aur kaam se lautkar ghar aana
Sabse khatarnaaq hota hai/ humare sapnon ka mar jaana

It's most dangerous/ to be filled with the silence of a corpse
To not feel anything/ to tolerate everything
To leave home for work/ and to return home from work
It's most dangerous/ when our dreams die

I also held dear a quote from *Lust for Life*, that I had bought for ten rupees at a book stall outside Punjab University—'*After all, the world is still great.*'

With this book and a letter from the maverick filmmaker Arun Kaul, who had, at the time, produced a few programmes for Doordarshan, including the brilliant *Kashmir File*, I had arrived in Delhi in 1996. I started working with a newspaper in Jammu, but the earlier hardships we had witnessed in Jammu had left me bitter. I did not want to live there. So, I wrote a letter to Arun Kaul, and three weeks later, he replied. 'If you like my nose and I don't dislike your face, we might get along,' he said in his letter.

When we met at his residence, he told me, 'I can expect a Kashmiri Pandit to be anything—cowardly, sly, or arrogant. But he cannot be mediocre. It is just not in his genes. So rise up to your genes at least.'

I worked with him for six months, by which time *Kashmir File* had come to an end. Though I was still being paid a salary, there was hardly any work. And I still wanted to learn and so I quit my job.

In June 1997, I was still struggling to find another job and I was penniless. On June 13, a fire broke out in Delhi's Uphaar cinema and fifty-nine people lost their lives. The next day, Ravi called me. 'I just got a little worried; I called to check if you were all right,' he said. I said that I was.

Even in that penury, I really thought I was all right. *Struggle.* The word seemed so romantic. I had something of a support system in the city, though—a girl older than me and in love with me. She lived in a working women's hostel. I also had a friend who wrote software programs for a living and read Bertrand Russell at night.

At 4 a.m. on June 16, the phone rings. I wake up, startled. I answer it. And . . .

I have no recollection of what happened during the next three hours. At 7 a.m., though, I remember rushing to the women's hostel to meet the girl. The guard knows me. He smiles. 'So early today?' he asks. She comes out; she is annoyed—I woke her up so early. I tell her what has happened. I think, she will say something now. *Now, now she will hold my hand. Now, now I will cry.* But she says nothing. She does nothing. She nods sympathetically and suppresses a yawn. 'I'll leave,' I say. I run to my friend's house. I knock. He opens the door. There is a razor in his hand, he is shaving. I tell him. *Now, now: one embrace. Now, now he'll make me sit down. Now, now he'll ask what I am going to do.* But nothing. He keeps shaving his chin. 'It's God's will,' he says. I run away.

I remember an incident Ma had narrated to me. My parents had recently married, and along with my uncle's family, they had gone to the Exhibition Grounds in Srinagar to watch a circus show. There was an artist who had climbed up on to a high platform where he was going to set himself afire and then jump into a pool of water below. But at the last moment he developed cold feet. He lit matchstick after matchstick, but he could not get himself to perform the act.

I became like that circus artist. I would make friends; we would eat, drink, joke. But I could never get myself to take that final plunge. I isolated a portion of my heart. I kept in it things I would share with no one. Like Nusrat Fateh Ali Khan's lines in *Bandit Queen*: *Khud se kahi jo kahi, kahi kisi se bhi nahi* (What I said to myself, I told no one).

That night I am alone on the bus to Jammu, in the last seat. They are showing *Khalnayak* on the bus. I am numb with pain.

At dawn, we cross the border of Jammu and Kashmir. At the Lakhanpur gate, I buy the *Daily Excelsior*. No, no, no, no. This is not Ravi. Why is there blood on his face? Why is his photo on the front page? So it is Ravi.

The previous day, Ravi left Jammu with two other Pandit colleagues for Gool. The summer vacations were over and I'd met him a fortnight ago. 'I am trying to be transferred to Jammu. Shubham is growing—he needs me,' he had told me. Just before Gool, the bus comes to a halt and armed men enter. They have specific information about three Pandits on board the bus. Ravi knows what this means. He hugs the other two men. They are asked to step out of the bus, which leaves without them. Ravi tries to fight the men. He is hit in the face. All three of them are shot. That midnight, the police come knocking at the door of Ravi's house in Jammu. His father opens the door. They tell him. The police want no trouble. The family is asked to cremate the bodies as quickly as possible.

I reach Jammu. Ravi is dead. My brother is dead, my hero is dead. Strangely, the only memory that comes back to me is of the time we went to Shalimar Garden and saw that green-haired foreigner.

Ravi is dead. Life is empty. Family is meaningless. Ma never recovers. I think it is from that moment onwards that she began to slip away. Ravi's father never recovered. He kept saying: '*Ye gav mein kabail raid'e*—this is my personal tribal raid.'

The tribal raid. When invaders from Pakistan came and destroyed what my maternal grandfather had built. That is my maternal uncle's story—of his losses when he was just ten. That story is very much a part of our exile. I will let Ravi's father tell you that story. In his own voice.

PART FOUR

*A*fter Ravi's death, things fell apart. The family began to disintegrate. In a few months, Asha shifted elsewhere with Shubham. Ravi's mother spent the hours endlessly watching television. She refused to take medicines for her diabetes and high blood pressure. A crazy restlessness crept into Ravi's father. He would visit us sometimes in Delhi, making an overnight journey, and after an hour or two had passed, he would get up and say he wanted to go back. It would take us hours to convince him to stay for at least one day.

In the summer of 2001, he came to Delhi. We had recently shifted house. He had a vague idea of where we lived. Without informing us, he landed on our doorstep one morning. He had made an overnight journey from Jammu. We were quite surprised at how he was able to locate the house. 'I just saw a towel hung over the clothes line in the balcony; I reckoned it must be yours,' he said. By the evening, of course, he was making noises about returning to Jammu the next day.

I remember the exact moment when Ravi's father began to tell me the story of the tribal raid of 1947. To prevent him from leaving the next day, I hid his bag in my room. He came looking for it, and ran his eyes over my bookshelf. I remembered a story I had heard from my mother—how he had a huge collection of books and how some of them were stolen by a cousin who sold them off to buy cigarettes. I mentioned this to him. 'Who told you this?' he asked, and his eyes shone and he slipped into a reverie. I was silent, avoiding looking at him so as not to make him conscious. 'You know, I came to Delhi for the first time in the 70s; I think it was 1976 . . .'

When I came to Delhi for the first time, I felt so lost. It was a January afternoon, I think in 1976, when the bus came to a halt somewhere in the middle of a vegetable market, and the conductor of the bus shouted that we had arrived in Dilli. I was the last man to get off the bus. As I climbed down the steps near the exit of the bus, the conductor smiled at me, and I thought that he had noticed my trembling legs. 'Don't worry,' he said to me with a grin, 'this is your own city; a man from your land ruled here till a few years ago, and now his daughter is its empress.' I was so taken aback by the crowds that I forgot what Jawaharlal Nehru, the man the bus conductor was referring to, looked like. I forgot his long aristocratic nose, the trademark of a Kashmiri. I forgot how he had appeared to me, almost thirty years ago when he climbed onto a wooden platform erected specially for him, in Lal Chowk, and addressed his own people— the people of Kashmir. I was then a young boy of ten, and I was a refugee.

And now, Nehru was dead. Hundreds of miles away from the familiar spaces of Lal Chowk, I was jostling for a foothold amidst a sea of people, and it seemed to me that they were coming at me from all sides. I somehow managed to get away and sat on the pavement, keeping my bag beside me. I kept holding it, as I had been advised by a friend's father who had visited Delhi a few years ago and had his baggage stolen while he stopped to buy himself a bun. I was also hungry and thirsty but I did not move. I then remembered the lunch my wife, Mohini, had packed for me as I left home. I would have probably taken a bus back to Jammu first and then another to Kashmir, had Ahdoo not arrived then and taken me to his home.

Ahdoo was a friend who dealt in carpets, who had, five years ago, extended his business to Delhi. Since then, he had invited me numerous times to visit him, and it was when he became a father that I finally accepted his offer and travelled beyond Kashmir for the first time in my life. In three days, I was back home, eating the turnips cooked by my wife.

It has been almost thirty years since that trip, but I still hold my bag when I visit Delhi. Though it does not matter where I live now. Delhi or the Deccan, it is all the same to me. No land is my land now.

When I saw Nehru for the first time in Lal Chowk, I was a refugee in my own state. Sixty years later, I am a refugee in my own country.

Sometimes, when I am alone, I almost hear Arnimal sing her lines to me: *Lass'e kami'e hawasay, maazas gaum basbasay.* There is no reason for me to live, I am just withering away.

Mohini, my wife, lives with me in a refugee settlement. She deserves a medal for living. One of her kidneys is damaged. She is diabetic. She has lost vision in her right eye.

After Ravi's death, I cannot stay in one place for long. I go and visit my daughter in Chandigarh. No sooner have I removed my shoes than I have this urge to run away. I go to my sister's house in Delhi. But from there as well, I feel like running away. It is only here, in the one-room dwelling of this refugee settlement, that I accept my destiny.

Every morning, I get up and read the newspaper. I always skip the first page. It carries the same news items, day after day. Like soggy peanuts, they are fried and made crisp and then served with catchy headlines for extra flavour. The second page carries a few pictures, and a few lines underneath each picture. The obituaries.

Prabhavati Kaul—originally from Habba Kadal, Srinagar—passes away in Janipura, Jammu.

Mohan Lal Dhar of Baramulla died on Monday in Talab Tillo, Jammu. Tenth-day rites at the Rajinder Park, Canal Road.

His ears still reverberating with the sound of the roaring waters of the Jhelum, Mohan Lal's tenth-day kriya will be performed in the dirty and characterless waters of the canal.

A priest has been called for conducting Mohan Lal Dhar's kriya ceremony. He is in a hurry, and he makes this clear, before even beginning to recite shlokas in his adenoidal voice. Rice has been cooked on a kerosene stove, and small mounds are made. Immersed in water up to his knees, the son breaks the creation of a potter over his shoulder. Then he takes a quick dip in the shallow water.

Every day, after going through the second page, I decide not to read the newspapers anymore. It makes me feel like Chitragupt—the clerk in the office of the lord of death, Yama—who maintains the records of life and death. I feel guilty, as if my reading the newspaper causes these deaths. But so far I have not stopped reading them. It is because of a sense of duty—of attending the death ceremonies and kriyas of people known to me.

On the banks of the canal, people with probably the same sense of duty have gathered to register their presence. Soon they form small groups and break into various discussions. The Kashmir situation, to begin with.

'Vajpayee's government has done nothing for us. Its Kashmir policy has been the worst so far.'

'Arre Dhar sahab, have you heard this—Chaman Lal Bhat's daughter has married a Bengali boy.'

'*Mahra*, it is a common trend now. Bengalis, Punjabis, Madrasis, Marathis—our children are marrying across India.'

'Forget it, friend. Tell me, what is your son upto, these days?'

'He has just completed his B.Tech, and is now pursuing an MBA from Pune.'

'Your sister's son—I heard he is a manager in a software company in Delhi. My sister-in-law's daughter, she has a BE in electronics—drawing a five-figure salary in a multinational firm. The family has their own house in Noida. Maybe both of them can click.'

The priest is looking at his watch at regular intervals. After he finishes this task, there is another in the offing—a Yagnopavit ceremony. Hymns are being fired like salvos. Even if the priest forgets to recite a couple of them, it would not matter. If the soul is pure, it will go to heaven. And if it is not, how can a shloka or two salvage the soul? The entire *Dharmashastras* would be of little help in that case.

Anyway, the ceremony is over, and so is a chapter called Mohan Lal Dhar.

When a person dies, the ghost of the deceased hovers around his mortal remains, and mourns for those he has left behind. To rouse dispassion in the ghost, the son to whom he is greatly attached performs the *Kapal-Kriya*—the breaking of his skull.

Who will rouse that dispassion in me?

It is said that the heaviest load in this universe is that of a father carrying his son's body. Ask me, I have carried it myself and my shoulders are still bent. It was I who took a dip in the same canal water on my son Ravi's tenth-day kriya, and then on the eleventh day, through the efficacy of mantras sent his soul to the abode of my ancestors.

My condition is much like that of the king of Nagrama—now Nagam Tehsil, where I served as a teacher, many years ago.

Damudhar, as he was called, built his kingdom, Satrasteng, on a plateau and also had a dam constructed for water. One day, as he prepared to leave for a bath, he was stopped by Brahmins, who asked for food. But the king refused, saying he would have his bath first and then feed them. Angered by the king's refusal, the Brahmins cursed him, turning him into a snake. The legend says that the snake can still be seen in search of water. He is not to be freed from the curse until he hears the whole *Ramayana* recited to him in a single day.

How will I seek my salvation? Who will recite the *Ramayana* for me?

Baramulla, 1947

Every story has a character who plays a significant role. But I have been a mere spectator, being forced to play my part beyond my free will.

Recently, one of the national magazines published a story on Kashmir. They interviewed me, asking me how I was coping with life after the death of my son. In the story, I was called 'the septuagenarian Prithvi Nath', but frankly, all these years seem to have passed like a flash of lightning.

Like a torrent, my memory washes away the years, to that moment when, perched in a walnut tree, I plucked raw, green fruit from the branches. That was the year 1947. India had just attained its independence. But nothing had changed in Kashmir. Maharaja Hari Singh was still the ruler of the land, and of our destinies.

Baramulla was still a lively town then—a transit point for English sahibs and mems, travelling in elegant Victorian-era cars, from the dusty roads of Rawalpindi to the elysian environs of Srinagar.

The Jhelum River passed through the town and then was joined by the muddy waters of the Kishanganga, before it flowed across, to the Pakistani mainland.

More than a thousand years ago, a Kashmiri engineer named Suyya concluded that floods in the valley occurred because the gorge near Baramulla was too narrow to handle the volume of the Jhelum. To solve the problem, Suyya hit upon a novel idea. He threw a large number of coins into the river. This led men to jumping into the waters to retrieve the coins. That, in turn, resulted in the removal of the boulders responsible for blocking the water. Later, during the Dogra king Maharaja Pratap Singh's rule, when a British residency had been established in the Valley, Major de Lotbiniere imported dredgers from America and an engineer from Canada, to do the same job.

I must have been around ten years old, I remember, when I crossed that old bridge in Baramulla to go across the town. My family was small by those days' standards—Father, Mother, my two younger sisters and me. In the middle of our house's courtyard, there was a well. It was known throughout the town for its sweet water. My father was poor, but he had a taste for good things. Our house was three-storeyed, and the top storey comprised a big hall. Huge wooden pillars supported the ceiling of the hall, and its many windows invited in the fresh, invigorating air.

My sisters were young. They stayed at home, while I went to the local Paathshaala everyday, wearing slippers, and carrying a slate in my hand. The school was a few miles away from home.

Father was always busy, but his younger brother—we called him Totha—always pampered us. In the morning, he would take me to the milkman to buy milk. Afterwards, he would ask the milkman to dole out a dollop of curd on my palm.

Totha took me on long walks and narrated to me so many stories about Kashmir. He told me how, about a hundred years ago, famines had led to an acute scarcity of food, forcing many families to settle in Lahore. He also told me how the famine of 1877 in Srinagar lasted for two years and drastically reduced the city's population. They used to say during the famine: '*Drag tsalih ta dag tsalih na.*' The famine goes but the stains remain.

One of Totha's friends was a man called Maqbool Sherwani. He was an activist in Sheikh Abdullah's party, the National Conference, and I often saw him riding a white horse. He visited our home often, to speak to Totha. Life was good.

One October morning in 1947, I woke up with a pain in my back. It so happened that while sleeping, I had shifted from the thick mattress, onto the floor. The floor, covered only with a thin mat, had made my back sore. I had a bath with hot water, on my mother's advice, and felt much better. Soon, I was walking towards my school as usual. When I reached, the morning prayers were in progress and I silently joined the line for my class. In front of me stood my friend Manzoor. I touched his shoulder and he turned to look at me. When he saw me, he took a step away from me and said, 'Prithvi, I need to tell you something after the prayer.'

'What is it, tell me now,' I said curiously. But before he could say anything, our class teacher walked by and Manzoor shut his mouth, while I quickly closed my eyes.

After the prayers, the children rushed to their classrooms. Manzoor ran towards the back of the school, and I followed him. He stopped under a tree.

'What is it that you want to tell me, Manzoor?' I asked him.

He was silent for a while and then, lifting a stone from the ground, began scratching something into the tree trunk.

'Manzoor, is it a joke you're playing on me? Tell me, what is it?' I said, my patience giving way.

Manzoor looked into my eyes with intensity. 'The Kazakhs are coming,' he said, almost vehemently.

'Kazakhs! Who are they? Why are they coming to Baramulla?'

'I don't know,' Manzoor said as he threw the stone. 'Let us go to the classroom, otherwise the teacher will whip us with nettle grass.' And he ran towards the class, while I tried to figure out what he meant. A minute later, having failed to understand what he was talking about, I followed him to class.

During the lunch break, I tried to find Manzoor, but he was not to be seen anywhere.

By the time I reached home, it was early evening, and I had forgotten all about Manzoor's revelation. After a meal of rice and fish curry, I went off to play. By the time I returned, the sun had dropped low in the sky, and it was beginning to get dark. I was very tired, and after helping myself to another serving of rice and fish, I went off to sleep.

As I was slipping away into sleep, I heard a knock on the front door and, from the sounds coming from the other room, I understood that Father had returned. I knew he would wash himself, and sit down to eat his dinner. Father preferred to eat at home. So when he returned, he would always be hungry. I heard Father and Mother speaking to each other.

Suddenly, I was startled awake by a shrill cry. At first, I thought I was dreaming, but after a few moments, I could clearly hear a commotion outside my house. I threw the quilt aside and ran out, barefoot and rubbing the sleep from my eyes, and saw that a few people had assembled in our neighbour's courtyard. In the middle of the courtyard our neighbour's son, Shyamlal, sat on the ground. He was wailing and beating his chest.

'What happened? Is all well with your family? Where is your father?' my father asked him.

Shyamlal did not answer. He kept wailing. 'Everything will be destroyed. Everything will be reduced to ashes. *Thrath ha se peye*—lightning has stuck us!'

'Stop this. Tell me clearly what has happened,' Father said.

'The Pathans are coming, the Pathans. They will kill us and take everything.'

'Are you sure you are not feverish? Pathans? What on earth are you talking about?'

'They are coming. This is not gibberish; they are coming from there,' Shyamlal pointed towards the mountains. 'They are coming to loot and kill us.'

The news spread like wildfire. Men came out of their homes, onto the streets, forming small groups, and discussed this new development. In no time, the news spread that Pakistan had sent tribal invaders from their Northwest Frontier Province to attack Kashmir. We soon learnt that the invaders had already wreaked havoc in the villages near the Uri township, and now they were advancing towards Baramulla. It would take just a few days, or maybe even less, for them to reach and attack Baramulla.

The thought of invaders sent shivers down the spines of people throughout Baramulla. Everyone was in a dilemma, and it was writ large on their faces—Would they have to leave their homes and run away? Would it be insane to stay? Or did it make sense to flee to Srinagar? Nobody had a clue.

Shambhu Nath made his stand clear.

'I cannot leave Lakshmi here. In her condition, it is not possible to take her to Srinagar.' Lakshmi was Shambhu Nath's cow and she was pregnant.

The shadow of fear loomed large over us, eclipsing the tranquillity of the town. In difficult times, everyone thinks about their own kith and kin. In no time at all, a few houses were found to have been locked up. These families had fled to unknown destinations, without telling anyone. A man who lived in the street behind ours lamented that his own brother's family had not even informed him before fleeing.

People who stayed back huddled inside their houses, taking extra precautions to lock the doors. Nobody could sleep. Families kept some of their valuables, mostly jewellery, ready, in case they had to flee. A few men kept kitchen knives under their pillows, so that they could put the womenfolk to death in case the tribesmen attacked.

It was then that a man came to our rescue. He was a senior officer at the Mahura power station, and the only Kashmiri Pandit in Baramulla who owned a car. He was middle-aged, and carried a baton in his hands. He was often seen walking past St. Joseph Chapel. The next morning he called for a meeting of members of the Pandit community.

Many people assembled at the school grounds to hear him. He was seated on a cane chair, a shawl draped carelessly over his shoulders.

'Look, things are not going to work this way. You are unnecessarily creating panic. I have thought about it, and I think I know what needs to be done,' he said. Everyone sat silent, looking at him.

'I have decided that I will go to the Mahura power station. If the Pathans are coming towards the town, they will have to cross Mahura. If I spot them, I will cut off the electric supply. That will be the signal for you to run away to safety.'

The idea seemed acceptable to all. Mahura was quite far and from there it would take the Pathans some time to reach Baramulla.

'But I have heard that they are not Pathans but Kazakhs,' said someone.

'It does not matter who they are. Remember one thing, they are outsiders. Everyone outside Kashmir has his eyes set upon this land. They want to molest Kashmir. They want to loot it. If they had their way, they would turn the course of the Jhelum. They would want to turn this land into a desert,' he responded.

And then he rose to leave.

'Keep an eye on the power supply,' he said as he drove away. Soon his car became invisible, leaving behind only a trail of dust.

Men went back to their homes to tell their families about the officer's plan. The roads turned desolate. I heard a baby crying somewhere, but the sound stopped so suddenly that I thought his family must have stifled the cries. Girls stopped playing hopscotch in the streets and boys could no longer be seen climbing trees.

Who could cook and who could eat in such circumstances? Mother boiled some rice, and my sisters and I ate some with a piece of onion pickle. Father and Mother ate nothing. Father recited some hymns softly. In between, he would look up at the lightbulb. Afterwards, he just kept staring at it, with Mother sitting next to him. The fear, coupled with anxiety, had become unbearable.

Later that evening, the lights went off.

Jaayen to jaayen kahan . . . Whenever I hear this melancholic song by Talat Mahmood, I am reminded of that October evening in Baramulla. The lights went off and with them, our hopes were extinguished too.

There was absolute chaos in the town. Shambhu Nath set Lakshmi free, as he prepared to flee to safety with his family. There were tears in his eyes as he put a tilak on Lakshmi's forehead and garlanded her. As he patted her, he was inconsolable. Finally he folded his hands in respect and left without looking back. Lakshmi followed her master for a while, but then stopped. With a calf in her womb, she stood exhausted, her legs trembling.

Father decided to move us to another village, where one of his acquaintances happened to live.

'Ambardar will give us shelter,' he said. Mother packed the previous night's leftover rice and a few pieces of onion pickle in a muslin cloth. After locking the house, we set off towards Ambardar's village.

Confusion reigned on the roads. Families ran helter-skelter to safer places. Most of them set off on the road to Srinagar. A few families hired houseboats that would take them to Srinagar via the river route. Some of them fled to nearby areas like Sopore, assuming that the tribesmen would not strike there. They took along with them household items like carpets, utensils, and bedding. Some of them carried the idols of their deities in wooden boxes. I saw an old man holding his hookah under his arm. A young girl cried over the shoulder of her father. A rag doll had fallen from her hand, and her father would not even stop to pick it up.

I carried my youngest sister on my shoulders. Father wore a long overcoat, and a pair of imported leather shoes, which had been gifted to him by an Englishman for whom he had prepared a horoscope. In one of the inside pockets of his overcoat, he put a few coins. It was the only money he had.

In the moonlight, the tall, lean poplar trees appeared to touch the sky. On the way, we saw a number of families moving in the same direction as us. At first they would be frightened at the sight of other people, and then, without exchanging a word, they would keep moving. Apart from a few household items, families carried with them their hopes of returning home soon.

The sun was about to rise, and the sky had turned a pale orange towards the east when we reached Ambardar's village.

Ambardar's house was like a mansion—it had a huge wooden door with iron handles, broad verandas and high windows. Ambardar himself was a towering personality—tall, broad-shouldered, with a long face. Around sixty years old, Ambardar wore several rings on both hands and always carried a walking stick with him which had a carved lion's face as its handle. He owned several orchards and many acres of land.

Ambardar welcomed our family with open arms. He too had heard the news of tribesmen advancing towards Baramulla.

'They won't be able to reach this far,' he said.

Like us, many other families known to Ambardar had taken refuge in his house. After walking all night, we were very tired. My legs were shaking with exhaustion. We washed ourselves at a small stream flowing beside Ambardar's fields.

The upper storey of his house had a huge room that was used for storing fruit from his orchards. We were told to help ourselves, as it was difficult to cook food for so many people. The children went first, followed by the adults. We pounced upon the fruits, and ate them to our hearts' fill. We ate pears, apples, and walnuts. We slept on haystacks, under old blankets and quilts that Ambardar provided for us.

We children were quite scared of Ambardar, but he would pay no heed to us. He would pass us occasionally, as we tried to play a few games with other children, in front of the house. He would talk to the elders though. I often noticed him removing dead leaves and other blockages from the water channels going towards his fields.

After three days, we realized how short our stay at Ambardar's house was to be. It so happened that a planter working in Ambardar's fields heard news of the tribesmen ransacking the main township of Baramulla. He also told Ambardar that the tribesmen were fanning out across villages, looting and plundering whatever they came across.

Many houses in the village belonged to Muslims. Some of them were landlords, and some worked in the fields and shared the crops with the owners. The news of the Pathans creating havoc in Baramulla spread like wildfire through the village. Ambardar shared this information with the heads of the families who had taken refuge in his house. Upon hearing the news, a lady, whom I remembered as generally being very quiet, broke down.

'Where will we go now? Oh God, strike me dead. It is much better than finding ourselves amidst these devils from across,' she cried, as her two children sat bewildered at her feet. The other women tried to console her.

As the men sought each other's opinion on what options were available to them, my father took charge.

'I propose that we stay here for now. Let me go and find out what the mood in the village is like. Depending on my findings, we will decide what is best for our safety,' Father said.

Normally the rest would have argued. But this time fear had sewn their mouths shut. This time they just nodded in agreement. Father put on a skullcap he borrowed from one of Ambardar's Muslim workers and went out to assess the risk of staying in the village.

On the streets, people moved in groups. Some of them were coming out of the village mosque after offering prayers. Outside a shop, a few men stood talking to each other. Father joined them. A man among the group was telling the others, 'The Pathans have reached Baramulla. They are planning to advance towards Srinagar. I have been told that they have plans to offer prayers at the Jama Masjid in Srinagar.'

An old man who was in the group said, 'They have ruined us. They are slaughtering innocent people.'

'But they are only killing infidels,' the first man replied.

The old man said nothing.

'Let us just wait and watch,' someone else said. Afterwards, the group dispersed.

Father told us later that as he was walking away, someone had caught his hand from behind. He turned to see a man standing there. He smiled at my father and said, 'Pandit, I know you are from Baramulla. A cousin of mine stays near your house. Listen, these antics won't help. I am telling you, your lives are in grave danger. Run away as soon as you can. May Allah be with you.' Then he left.

The news Father brought back with him was not encouraging.

'I really don't know what to do; nothing is clear,' Father told the others.

Now the question was whether to stay put, or move ahead to some other village. The men arrived at the collective decision that they should hide in Ambardar's fields. The invaders, they thought, would not be able to find them there. Father went to Ambardar and asked him to join the rest for safety, but he declined.

'Son, throughout my life, I have never slept anywhere outside my house. Now why should I change that in my old age? Don't worry about me. The greh devtaa will protect me. But you carry on, if you must.'

Greh devtaa. Ghar divta. I look at Ravi's father. He sits there in front of me, his head trembling slightly. I am reminded of that morning in 1990 when we left our house forever, and how Father had turned back to invoke the greh devtaa to protect our house.

I tell Uncle about my nightmare in 1987 when I saw a marauder, wearing sandals of dry straw, plunging his sword into Ravi's abdomen. His eyes well up with tears. He doesn't say anything about Ravi. 'So Ambardar stayed back, while we walked towards the fields,' he continues.

There were twenty-nine of us who hid in the fields that night. The children were asked to not make any noise and just lie still with their parents.

The head of one particular family was a man in his mid-thirties and, like a traditional Brahmin, he maintained a tuft of hair at the back of his head. He asked me if I could procure a pair of scissors or a knife from somewhere. I got hold of a blunt knife and upon his request, I cut off the tuft of hair. He took it from me and buried it under a tree, tears flowing down his cheeks.

The night was horrifying. As we braved the cold out in the open, I could hear the distant howling of jackals. Most of us remained awake. Those who dozed off would wake up every now and then after dreaming that the tribesmen had caught them. A mother tried to sing a lullaby to her restless child, but was asked to shut up by her husband. Another woman buried a ring under a tree. 'My mother gave me this ring while she was dying. I don't want the Pathans to take it away,' she said.

It was around midnight, when suddenly the sound of gunfire reverberated in the air. The howling of jackals died away. We could hear cries from one corner of the village, followed by more gunshots.

We got up instantly, all of us, unsure of what to do. The cries seemed to be nearing us, and this took our courage away.

'What do we do now?' asked a man.

'Let us run away to the next village or the village next to that. But we must leave now,' my father said.

So twenty-nine of us, six families altogether, began to run. Initially, all of us stayed together. But gradually, the families could not keep pace with each other. Some of them slowed down due to exhaustion and some drifted away. I followed my father, who was carrying my sister on his back by now. My eyes were heavy with stress and fatigue. My chest had turned into a furnace, but stopping could have meant death.

By the wee hours of the morning, our family was the only one that reached the outskirts of a village. We did not know what the situation would be there, so we decided to hide until morning in an orchard nearby. On one end, by the roadside, there stood a row of willows. Beyond them were paddy fields where the crop was ripe for cutting.

It must have been late in the morning when we came out of hiding, treading each step with caution. While walking, Father and I tried to listen for sounds of chaos coming from the village but we could hear none.

We must have walked half a mile or so when we came across a man working in a field. Upon hearing our footsteps, he turned towards us. He stared at us for a few moments and then resumed his work. We also did not try speaking to him. Those were terrible times, and one was not sure whom one could trust. As we crossed him, I noticed that he was stealing glances at us. I told this to my father in a hushed tone.

'Don't look at him; just keep on moving,' Father said. And so I did.

We kept walking through the fields, avoiding roads. We had no destination in mind. Our only aim was to get as far away from the tribesmen as we could.

We must have walked for an hour or so when we heard someone calling out my father's name. We turned to see a woman with a sickle in her hand. Father recognized her.

'I don't remember her name but her husband used to work in Ambardar's fields,' father said.

We walked towards her and as we neared her, she said, 'Damodar Pandit, is that you?'

'Yes, it is me. We are coming from Ambardar's village. The tribesmen attacked in the night.'

'And what about him?' she enquired about Ambardar.

Father told her about Ambardar's decision to stay back.

'*Ha Khudaya*, does he not know that these evil Pathans are baying for the blood of Kashmiris? More so when one happens to be a non-Muslim? But he won't listen to anyone. You are of his own tribe. You should have made him realize his folly.'

Father said nothing. She dropped her sickle on the ground and cleaned her mud-caked hands on her smock. After asking us to wait there, she disappeared. She returned after a minute or so with a pitcher of fresh milk in her hands. The milk was so fresh that even the froth had not settled.

'Here, at least feed these young children,' she said as she gave the milk to my mother.

We were famished, and all of us drank straight from the pitcher. After my mother's milk, if I am indebted to anything, it is the milk provided that day by the kind woman.

Father realized that we had come very far from our home. There was no place left where we could seek refuge. Also, there was no guarantee that we would not be forced to run from that village also. Father decided that it was time to go back to Baramulla, to our home.

'Let us go home. Whatever has to happen, will happen. We cannot change destiny,' he said.

'Do you realize how risky it could be?' Mother almost shouted at Father.

'There are a few things which should be left to God, Shobha,' Father said. 'We have tried our best to save ourselves; we cannot go further than this. There is no point. If God wishes that we should return to him then so be it. We must surrender to the will of God.'

And so we began our return journey. On the way back, we realized that people were still fleeing from their villages. People from the neighbouring township of Uri, which had borne the brunt of the marauders, told harrowing tales of the tribesmen's attack.

A woman howled while walking through a field with a child following her. He was crying too. We learnt that the woman's husband, a shopkeeper in Uri, had been killed by the tribesmen after a group broke into their house. I was terrified when I saw a thin line of blood running down her thighs where her dress was torn. It was torn near her chest too. But she was oblivious to everything now. She was crying and pulling her hair. A woman from her neighbourhood was trying to console her. She was also trying to cover her with a shawl but the woman threw it away repeatedly.

'The workers of the National Conference were trying to stop people from leaving Uri. They said nobody would touch us. But before they could even finish, the Pathans descended upon our town and we just ran blindly amidst a volley of bullets,' a man from Uri told Father.

We had walked a few miles when we saw another horde of people approaching. They were almost running. They looked at us and one of them shouted, 'Run away, run away. They are coming in this direction.'

A cry of panic escaped my mother's lips and Father hurried us towards the fields along the road. We ran deep into the fields, hoping to find a village where the tribesmen had not entered. As we ran, we were joined by a couple. After a few miles, we stopped to take stock of our situation and catch our breaths. The couple stopped, too. The woman was tall and fat, with a round face, while her husband was lean and had a long face. The man told us that the tribesmen had attacked their village, which was across the bridge in Baramulla and he had fled with his wife, leaving his aged father, who was paralysed, behind.

'Don't worry,' my father tried to reassure him, 'they will not harm your father.'

'No, brother, you don't know them,' the man replied. 'They are thirsty for blood, worse than mongrel dogs. They might kill my father because one of his teeth is made of gold. Oh God, I should have at least knocked out his tooth before running away to save my life.' The man was crying now.

It was only later that we realized the truth of what the man had told us. When the Pathans set foot on the soil of Kashmir, they nursed a desire to lay their hands upon as much gold as they could. Their eyes blinded with greed, the tribesmen could not even distinguish between brass and gold. Brass was the metal that Kashmiris used the most. Brass plates to eat food, brass tumblers and *khasoos* to drink water and tea, and brass spoons to rekindle simmering coals in kangris. Even the bases of hookahs and toothpicks were made of brass. All this was taken away by the Pathans. And even gold teeth from people's mouths, before putting them to death.

We kept walking, accompanied by the couple. The woman, I noticed, was carrying a bundle, which she held under her arm. There was no one in sight as far as the eye could see. Only trails of smoke appeared in the distant sky.

'They have plundered Baramulla,' the man remarked. 'Nothing is left for us to go back to.' We looked hopelessly towards the sky. Above us, eagles circled.

The sun was shadowed by clouds, which made the surroundings even more depressing. Mother's feet were swollen and she was finding it difficult to walk. She held Father's shoulder for support.

Eventually we came across two hillocks overlooking a huge, barren field. We hoped that there might be a village beyond the hillocks where we could take refuge for a few days before continuing our journey towards Baramulla. But before we could proceed, the sound of gunfire shook us. Birds flew out of the trees, scattering leaves weakened by autumn. We could not escape now. The tribesmen were somewhere near us.

'Don't panic,' Father muttered and then he began to say loudly, '*Allah ho Akbar!*' My heart beat furiously. Mother's face turned pale. The woman rushed towards my younger sister. 'Keep this under your pheran,' she said, handing her bundle to my sister. No sooner had she done this than we saw three tribesmen descending from a hillock towards our left. '*Allah ho Akbar, Allah ho Akbar,*' my father kept repeating loudly. One of the tribesmen said something in Punjabi and signalled us to stop. We froze.

I could see the Pathans clearly now. They had long beards, dyed with henna. One of them wore a turban. His face was sunburnt. They wore sandals made of dried straw, and carried guns. One of them came forward and began frisking us. His two accomplices spread an embroidered bed sheet on the ground. They were looking for gold and other precious items that they suspected we were carrying. But the search disappointed them. The third tribesman was gazing at my sister. She must have looked nervous, as she was trying to hide behind Mother. The tribesman came forward and with the speed of a hawk lifted my sister's pheran. A cry escaped her lips, and the bundle fell down. As they opened it, I saw their eyes gleaming. They laughed demonically. Two of them clapped furiously while laughing with their faces turned upwards. I looked at the woman, whose fortune had just been snatched away. She was crying silently. There was a strange expression on my sister's face, as if she had committed a crime. The Pathans were shouting with joy, hurling expletives in their language. Suddenly, one of them lifted my sister in his arms and placed a kiss on her forehead. That was their way of thanking her.

One of the tribesmen then pointed at my father's shoes. At first, father did not understand. The Pathan shouted again and pointed again towards the shoes. This time it was clear. Father unlaced his shoes and handed them over to the Pathan. The Pathan put them on, leaving his straw sandals for father to wear. Then the three invaders moved on. After a little while, when we could no longer see them, Father threw away the sandals in disgust. The woman's tears had turned into sobs. Her husband was consoling her. No one from my family uttered a word.

Walking had become a habit. We had walked another mile or so when we were again confronted by a few Pathans. We raised our hands, while Father started chanting *Allah ho Akbar*. We were frisked again. But now there was truly nothing to offer. In frustration, the Pathans kicked the men, then carried on with their forward march. We had walked just a few steps when the Pathans shouted at us from behind. We stood transfixed in our places. One of them pushed my father, and took off his coat. Then with a wave of his hand, he signalled us to go. We moved on.

Father was muttering inaudibly and mother tried to console him, knowing that he was distraught because of the loss of the coat.

'Don't think too much about the coat. Thank God that at least they spared our lives,' Mother said. 'I am not mourning the loss of that wretched coat. I feel sorry for having lost the money I had put in the coat's pocket. I thought it would enable me to buy some food for the children once we reached home,' he said and then slipped into silence. I did not look at him, but I knew he was crying.

I don't know why, but Tathya's loss of his shoes, coat and a little money took me back to December 1990. We were in Bhagwati Nagar, and we had very little bedding. One evening, a neighbour came and told Father that a local politician was distributing blankets. Ma looked at me. 'Why don't you go there? Maybe we could get a blanket as well,' she said. I didn't want to do it. It reminded me of the embarrassment of that half tomato that had been thrust in my hand that June. 'I won't go,' I said. 'We badly require that blanket,'

Ma said. It frustrated me. I didn't want to go, but I could not ignore the helplessness I saw in my mother's eyes. And so I went. I stood in the queue. I got that blanket.

I should have kept that blanket; I should have kept it as a testimony of Ma's helplessness, of our exile.

'After facing the marauding tribesmen, Father changed his plan. The couple was still accompanying us,' my Uncle recalled.

'Let us go back to Ambardar's village; at least we will have a roof over our heads. God only knows the fate of Baramulla. Let us see if we can spend a few days with Ambardar and then move on home,' Father said.

After many hours of walking, we reached Ambardar's village. We walked with caution, taking measured steps. It was evening and the sky was overcast with grey clouds. We could barely see the streets and walked through slush.

Eventually we reached Ambardar's house and saw that the main gate was half open. As Father opened it to let us enter, it made a strange, creaking sound. Two dogs that were sniffing at a bundle lying on the steps of Ambardar's house ran away. Father went forward and as he came close to the steps a cry escaped his lips. '*Om Namah Shivay*,' he invoked Lord Shiva. What we had thought was a bundle in the darkness was actually Ambardar's body. It lay on the second step, in almost a sitting position, with the head hanging backwards. Ambardar's walking stick lay at his feet, like a faithful dog. It seemed as though he would open his eyes, pick up his stick, and go out for a walk. But the blood on the stairs, which had turned black, narrated the truth. The tribesmen had sieved his body with bullets.

We were so tired that none of us could feel the grief of losing a friend, even one who had helped us in bad times.

'I want to die like him,' Father said pointing towards Ambardar's corpse. 'Let us go home. If we have to die, it makes sense to die like Ambardar. At least our blood will be absorbed in our own soil.'

Reciting ceremonial hymns, Father folded his hands. All of us folded our hands and turned back. Mother had put one corner of her sari in her mouth to muffle her sobs.

As for me, I could only hear Ambardar blessing me in his baritone voice: *Las te nav*—may you live long and prosper.

After we left Ambardar's village, the couple parted from us. We kept on walking towards home.

From a distance, we could see smoke emanating from our village. We walked, or rather limped with exhaustion, towards the street where our home stood. There were burnt houses all around, many of them still smoldering. A number of household items were strewn across the road. A child's frock. A brass tumbler. A few books. My father picked one up. It was Kalhana's *Rajatarangini*. There lay a wooden cupboard, with its door still locked. A pack of tobacco. A few pashmina shawls. One half-burnt carpet. One hookah, with its brass base ripped off. My father started reciting prayers. I could not understand why.

In a few minutes, we stood at the head of our street. Father looked at Mother, as if asking whether she had the courage to delve into the painful discovery of the fate of our home. Before we could take a step further, we heard a wail. We looked around. It was one of our neighbours. He started beating his forehead.

'Everything has been reduced to ashes, Damodar,' he cried.

The fire had spread in our locality after the invaders had entered and killed two sons of one of our neighbours. The boys had been asked to recite the Kalma by the marauders, but they had refused. The tribesmen had then shot them both. Their mother had then asked her husband to carry their bodies to the kitchen, to be cremated. The parents chose to burn alive along with their dead sons. The fire soon engulfed the house and then spread to the entire locality.

My mother could no longer stand on her feet. She sat on the road and sobbed. Father caught hold of my arm, and led me along the street to our home. On both sides of the street, houses were reduced to burnt stubs. We just kept walking. Here was our neighbour's house. The poor man had toiled for decades, and had lived a life of penury to build this house. Now it was gone.

And then we stood in front of what used to be our house. It had been devastated in the fire as well. Smoke still emanated from the window frames. All our belongings had been looted. My father walked slowly, as if he were walking in his sleep. He picked up a piece of dried turnip from the ground, and chewed on it. Then, as if he had gained energy from that dried turnip, he started rummaging through the debris. He was searching for something. I looked around our courtyard. For what seemed like hours, Father kept uttering something to himself as his hands kept working frantically, searching. He upturned bricks, stones and burnt wood. Finally he broke down. After a while, he paused and looked at me. He wiped his tears. 'I was looking for your grandfather's chillum. That is the last thing he touched before he left us.'

There was still no news of Totha when we boarded a tonga that would eventually take us to Srinagar. He was not at home when the news of the attack was broken to us.

My mother's head was resting on the wooden frame of the tonga, as she held one of my sisters in her lap. Father held my other sister, and I sat next to him.

Srinagar was fifty miles away. But for us, it was a leap to another world. From the security of a household to the uncertainty of a nomadic life. From light to darkness. From heaven to hell. We had no idea what lay in store for us once we reached Srinagar. From other fleeing families, we learnt that the Indian government had established refugee camps for those who came to Srinagar, escaping from areas like Baramulla, Sopore and Uri.

It was a dusty evening, and grey clouds, pregnant with water, held sway in the sky. Soon it started raining. Raindrops, each the size of a big pearl, started falling. Everyone ran for shelter. We took ours under the extended roof of a shop. Minutes before, the tongawallah had declared that we had reached Srinagar. Like our misfortune, the rain was also waiting for an appropriate moment to show that we were born when the gods had been looking the other way.

Volunteers of the National Conference were managing a few refugee camps, which had been set up in the heart of the city. Many Pandit volunteers from the city were helping as well with clothes, food and other essential items. We went to one of the camps where we were given a couple of blankets and a few handfuls of rice, which Mother held in a bundle fashioned out of one corner of her sari. This had to be cooked in community chullahs set up in the camp, using earthen pots provided by the government (though God knows which government was in command). Someone gave my sister a handful of dried brinjals. That evening, and for many evenings to come, we survived on rice and dried brinjals, turnips, onion, or just plain salt.

After we made the camp our temporary home, Father started searching for Totha. He checked every other refugee camp, hoping that he had reached Srinagar. He spoke to other families that came from Baramulla, but nobody seemed to have any clue about Totha. He had just disappeared. After some time, Father gave up. He thought that his brother had fallen to the bullets of the Pathans.

The sun-mottled streets of Srinagar brought no succour to our souls. The clouds of our despair were so thick, no ray of hope could penetrate them. The future was like a vast, barren landscape. We possessed nothing except memories of our home. We took stock of our battered selves, and began to plan for the times to come. Our first priority was to move out of the refugee camp. A fortnight after our arrival in Srinagar, we found a place. My father knew someone, who knew someone, who had a room available in his house in downtown Srinagar. In a locality known as Ganpatyar—the abode of Lord Ganpati, who resided in an ancient temple there.

Someone remarked to me later, and how right he was when I think of it, that the houses in Ganpatyar looked like sozzled men, leaning their heads on each others' shoulders. Only narrow, dark lanes, overflowing with filth separated them, with great effort. Gone were the days of living in airy rooms, supported by sturdy beams of wood. Rooms in Ganpatyar were dingy, with damp mud walls. We were given a room on the first floor. The kitchen was on the ground floor. It was a dreary, repulsive hole. There, the verses of Lal Ded would cause no compassion in hearts. No festival could ever be celebrated, no feast ever cooked. We lost our appetites. Not that there was much to cook.

In the front of the house was a small courtyard, which had never seen the sun. It was used for washing clothes and grinding spices in heavy stone mortars. Throughout the day, we could hear the landlady crushing red chillies, turmeric and cinnamon barks. Water for washing, cooking and bathing had to be carried from a public tap in one corner of the street. Women, carrying their dirty utensils in a wicker basket for washing, would assemble at the tap, and gossip about their husbands and mothers-in-law. My mother cried day and night. She feared that in that single dark room, without sun and air, her children would turn anaemic and die.

There was absolutely no work for Father. He tried seeking work in Srinagar, but the whole atmosphere was so gloomy that nobody celebrated anything, so his talents as an astrologer weren't needed for the moment. Even the dead were cremated in a hush, as if wailing over their bodies would result in the tribesmen gaining entry into Srinagar.

One could see men, their heads lowered, whispering silent prayers to the gods and beyond.

Then one day, Totha appeared. He had grown a beard and he wore a tattered pheran. Father hugged him and so did mother. She cried as well. Totha sat quietly in one corner and would not talk at all about where he had been for so many days. 'I am all right, don't worry,' he kept saying, but wouldn't tell us anything further. After a few days, he finally spoke about what had happened. He said he had been in hiding for days with volunteers of the National Conference. 'I've terrible news to share,' he said. 'Maqbool Sherwani is dead.'

When he learnt about the tribal invasion, Sherwani rode out on his horse, going from village to village, urging people, particularly the Pandits, not to leave. He had been galvanizing people to put up a brave front against the invaders. His party had coined a slogan to instill confidence among the people.

Hamlawar khabardaar, hum Kashmiri hein tayyar.

O invader beware, we Kashmiris are ready for you.

But when it became clear that the lives of many people were in jeopardy because thousands of tribesmen were approaching, he decided to sabotage their advance. For the invaders, reaching Srinagar was important and they were using local guides to show them the way. Through his network, Sherwani misguided the tribals, causing them to lose crucial time. But eventually, they saw through his trickery and captured him. He was dragged to a hillock where nails were hammered into his hands. Perhaps the marauders had taken a cue from the picture of Jesus Christ in St. Joseph's Chapel at the foot of the hillock. 'Victory to Hindu–Muslim unity,' Sherwani had shouted. A squad of invaders pumped bullets into his body and then nailed a piece of tin to his forehead. On it they had scribbled: 'A traitor deserves death as punishment.'

The marauders did not spare the chapel either. The chaplain, Colonel Dykes, believed the tribesmen would leave them untouched. 'Keep to the left and let them march,' he had assuredly told others in the chapel. But when the tribesmen arrived, they tore through the chapel and killed seven people, including Colonel Dykes and his wife Biddy Dykes who had given birth to their third son only days ago. Then the interior of the chapel was destroyed.

The tribesmen converted Baramulla's cinema hall into a rape house. Hundreds of women were taken there and raped. Some of them were later abducted and taken to Rawalpindi and

Peshawar and sold like cattle. Many women had jumped into
the Jhelum to save their honour.

A long while ago, one of my father's cousins had constructed a
house in Ganpatyar. For some reason, Father and his cousin
had not spoken to each other for years. I had no idea who he
was, until he saw me one day in the Ganpatyar temple. It was
my birthday, and Mother had asked me to visit the temple
to pray.

There were quite a few devotees in the temple that late
morning. The middle-aged priest, with his unshaven cheeks,
looked grim while distributing prasad. I had just taken the
offering from him, when I felt the tip of a stick tapping me on
my left shoulder. I looked around to see a man holding the
other end of the stick. With a bemused look on his face, and
almost suppressing a smile, he asked me, 'Are you Damodar's
son?'

Before I could answer, he spoke again. 'I have been told that
you are staying in that ramshackle house. The landlord is
shikaslad—a miser. His face is like the ruins that he calls his
house.' He paused, looking intensely into my eyes.

'Tell your father to leave his *trakjaar*—his stiff ego. Tell him
that I am his brother, though he has never bothered to check
whether I exist or not. Tell him that I will come later in the day,
to meet him and take you all to my house.' He patted my head
and left.

I ran like mad from the temple to our temporary home, to
break the news to my father. 'Which spirit has possessed you?'
the landlady yelled at me. She was coming out of the main gate

and I almost crashed into her as I was charging in. Without paying heed to her, I went inside, breathless.

Mother was cooking and Father was sitting on a seat of dry grass, reciting hymns. Immediately, I told Mother about my encounter in the temple. When I looked around, Father had stopped his recitation. He was looking at me, but it was obvious from the look on his face that he was lost in thought. There was silence for a while. The earthen pot set on the hearth whistled gently.

And then Mother spoke. 'You must go and buy some cardamom and cinnamon. If he comes, at least we should be able to offer him a *khasoo* of kahwa.'

Father did not say anything. I was thankful that I didn't tell him that his cousin had called him stiff. Without uttering a word, Father went out, and when he returned, besides the spices for kahwa, he had also got some hot bagels.

Father's cousin arrived just before noon. He wore a tweed pheran and a cream-coloured turban. He carried the same walking stick in his hands, and he coughed as he climbed the stairs. That was intended to serve as a signal to us, a signal that he had arrived. Father received him at the door, and they silently hugged each other. Mother served him steaming hot kahwa. Uncle held it with the right cuff of his pheran, and took a sip with a slurping sound. The fragrance of the kahwa spread throughout the entire room, burying the rancid smell of damp walls. The spiced tea appealed to Uncle's senses, and he closed his eyes, savouring his tea. Eventually, he put the *khasoo* down, and spoke. 'Why are you hell-bent on ruining my name?' he turned towards my father. 'People say that I have a big three-storeyed house to myself and my tenants, but I cannot accommodate my own cousin's family. It was one of our mutual

friends who pointed out your son to me, and that is how I met
him at the temple. Now for God's sake, leave your *trakjaar*, and
shift to my house.'

When I heard him calling my father stiff to his face, I thought
that there was no chance my father would relent. My father was
very proud, almost arrogant. But to my surprise, he replied in a
voice that could best be described as feeble. 'It is not my pride,
brother. These are hard times for all of us and I don't want to be
of any inconvenience to you.'

'It is no inconvenience to help one's own blood during distress.
Had it not been for these blood-mongers, you would never have
come to this wretched place. It is all Karma, my dear brother.
We are mere puppets in his hands,' said Uncle. Before he left, he
kissed my sisters and me, and put some cashews into our hands.

And so it happened that we shifted to uncle's house, two days
later. We hardly had any possessions that needed shifting—just
ourselves, and a few articles that were easy to carry by hand.

Our new house was situated on the banks of the Jhelum
River. Every morning, Father would go down to the freezing
river and, immersing himself up to his waist, he would recite
shlokas and offer water to the sun god with his copper pitcher.

I was admitted in a school in Srinagar. But I missed Baramulla
terribly. And Sopore, too. The apple town of Sopore, which
neighboured Baramulla, was where my father's sister lived, and
a place I had visited often. The family had fled from Sopore
during the attack, as we had fled from Baramulla, but upon
returning, they at least had found their house to be safe.

The air of Srinagar never suited me. So at the slightest
opportunity, I would escape to Sopore.

The harsh winter had passed, and tiny white blossoms began
to appear on the almond trees. Streams gurgled with the icy

waters of godly glaciers, and there was spring in the air. Kangris were still used by some. But most were content with the warmth provided by the sun.

I would return home from school and try to study. Mother kept busy with her domestic chores and taking care of my two sisters. Father had started teaching again, and drawing up horoscopes.

In school, I made some new friends. But my mind would always wander to Baramulla. And Sopore. The summer had not yet arrived when I took a few annas from my father and rushed to Sopore. My heart swelled with joy as the hustle-bustle of Amira Kadal gave way to the Sopore road, dotted with poplar trees on either side. Beyond the poplar trees stood vast apple orchards. When they bore their fruit, the fruits would be packed into wooden cases, and then sealed with dry straw. But for now, the trees stood bare, laden only with the expectations of their bounty.

A strange, and yet not so strange, peace prevailed upon me when the bus crossed the bridge over the Jhelum and entered Sopore. I could finally see the tonga stand, near the entrance of the town. As I alighted from the bus, the familiar scent of the town greeted my nostrils. My legs shook, and I ran towards my aunt's house. A bee flew along with me. I could hear its continuous buzzing. My cheeks must have become flushed from the running, as someone on the road teasingly called me an Ambur apple. An Ambur apple is one of the special Kashmiri apple varieties. I reached the main gate of my aunt's house and began shouting for my cousins. They were not expecting me, and were surprised when they saw me. I hugged them, and tears leapt from my eyes, and were lapped up by the hem of my aunt's dress. After a sumptuous lunch of rice, pumpkin and beans, I went with my cousins to the banks of the river.

The Jhelum was very wide here, and it roared as it neared a bend. We got busy, catching the river's colourful fish. Somewhere nearby, a group of hunters were trying to shoot down a flock of cranes, which they would later sell. This thought made me sad, because I was reminded of father getting its delicious meat when we were in Baramulla, before the misfortune of migration had struck us. This memory and its accompanying sadness cast a shadow of depression over my mind, and I cut myself away from the boys. I lay in the compound of Sopore's ancient temple, staring at the vast expanse of sky above. I heard a gunshot, and I knew someone would have a feast in the evening. I began to cry. After a while, I heard my cousins calling my name, but I didn't feel like answering.

I don't know when I slipped into sleep, but I did sleep at some point. And I only awakened from that sleep after eight months.

When my cousins could not find me, they informed my uncle that I was missing. He, along with other neighbours, was about to start looking for me, when the temple priest told them about a boy who had been found lying unconscious in the temple compound. That was me. I was dazed and hallucinating with fever. A doctor was summoned, and he prescribed a few medicines and cold packs. But I did not recover. For months, I kept slipping in and out of consciousness. The doctor eventually came to the conclusion that I was suffering from a rare form of fever, which would go away only with time. I don't remember much of that eight-month period, which felt like a long dream. I dreamt of my burnt-down house. I dreamt of that tribesman who had snatched the bundle of gold from my sister. I could hear the tribesman's laughter. I dreamt of Ambardar's stick. I dreamt that I was starving. I was later told that I cried often during that period.

When I finally opened my eyes, winter had already arrived. The first thing I saw from the window of my room was snowfall. Large but light flakes of snow fell from the sky, and froze in the chilly wind, turning the ground icy. Occasionally, I could hear the sound of a huge mass of snow falling from the slanting tin rooftops of houses. The mass would land with a noisy thud, as if the heavens were falling. Boys would pluck icicles from their windows and roofs and suck on them like ice lollies. My parents thanked God and the lungs of a sheep were offered to the goddess Kali, in gratitude for my revival.

I had lost a lot of weight during my illness. So I was fed with milk and cheese, and a lot of eggs. The first thing I said when I could speak was—I don't want to go back to Srinagar. Bowing to pressure and keeping in mind my fragile mental state, Father agreed to let me stay in Sopore and study there. This brought a mixed bag of emotions. On the one hand, I was elated that I could now stay in Sopore. I felt as if wings were borne out of my shoulders. But on the other hand, there was also a sense of rootlessness—a feeling that I would be away from my father's gentle but firm gaze, mother's lullabies and my sisters' innocent conversations. But I could not imagine myself living in those narrow lanes of Srinagar. The mere thought of it brought bile to my mouth.

It snowed so heavily that winter that the Sopore–Srinagar road was blocked. Labourers were hired by the state administration to clear the roads. No amount of work they did seemed adequate. Even as they cleared the snow from the road, a fresh fall would begin tracing its way down from the sky, into the depths beneath. The snow would freeze overnight.

Father got stuck in Sopore because of me. It took a week for the weather situation to ease. After taking a tonga halfway, walking in the snow for miles, then taking a bus, Father eventually reached Srinagar. I was later told that Mother wept inconsolably when she did not see me with Father and that she could not speak properly for days without tears overcoming her.

I began attending school, along with my cousins. In the morning, after a breakfast of milk and rotis made of rice flour, we would leave home for school, carrying our slates in our hands, and our books tied up in a cloth. Many times after school, when we went out to play, I would sneak alone into the compound of the temple, which was built on the banks of the Jhelum. I would lie down in the same place where I had slipped into oblivion months ago, with my face towards the sky. I got into the habit of looking at the clouds for hours, observing them as they took various shapes. Sometimes a cloud would be an elephant, sometimes a horse, sometimes a demon, and sometimes a fairy. And sometimes, when a wicked cloud assumed the shape of that tribesman, I would close my eyes against it, rise, and rush back home. I would try not to think about it.

The years passed by. I went to school, following more or less the same routine each year. I lived in Sopore, but I would visit Srinagar during winter vacations, and sometimes even during the summers.

During such visits to my parents' home in Srinagar, Mother would stuff me with the choicest dishes. Beans and dry turnips. Dried brinjals and a hotchpotch of rice and pulses. Uncle would treat me too, in his own way, putting cashews, chestnuts, and raw walnuts and almonds into my pocket.

During those visits to Srinagar, I began to notice that Father was getting some grey hair. He spoke very little, preferring to read the scriptures while sitting in a corner of a room. He had also developed a terrible temper, and had several times thrown a plate of rice across the room, just because he'd detected chaff amidst the rice grains, or a seed in a chilli that Mother had used to garnish a dish. I asked Father about this, one evening. He was silent for a long while. When he spoke at last, he said, 'You are young. When you grow up, then you will realize what pride is all about, and how essential it is for manhood.'

A few years later, I took the matriculation exams, and stood first in the entire Baramulla district. I was ecstatic. I was in Srinagar when the results were declared, but when I told Father, he just nodded his head. If he was happy, he did not show it. He kept his lips glued to his hookah. The only sign of his possible happiness and pride in my accomplishment was that after hearing the results, he pulled on his hookah a little harder than usual. My mother, though, went to the temple, and offered thanksgiving to Lord Ganpati.

My father decided that for a few months, I would work in a chemist shop run by a family acquaintance. I remember making a feeble attempt to protest against his decision that I work in Shamnath Tickoo's chemist shop. 'I don't want to work there,' I told him, looking at the ground near my feet.

I could feel father staring at me. He was writing a letter to someone, and though I didn't look at him, I knew that he had taken off his spectacles. They rested on his thigh, and he put his pen down, and finally spoke to me.

'Son, though you were young, I hope you remember that handful of coins those Pathans took away, along with my coat. It seems as if along with those coins, our luck has been abducted. No matter how hard we try, I don't think it will come back now.'

He cleared his throat, then continued.

'You know our circumstances, nothing is hidden from you. You know that I will not be able to support your education further. I am trying to secure a government job for you. I have requested some of my friends to try and arrange a job for you. Until that happens, you must work with Shamnath.'

I contemplated Father's words. He was right. Even when I registered for the matriculation exams, I had to seek help from a friend's family for my registration fees. My thoughts were interrupted by Father, who spoke again.

'Remember one thing, Prithvi. There is only one thing that will help us Kashmiri Pandits for years to come. No matter what happens, we must get ourselves government jobs, all of us. That is the only key to our survival now.'

Now, years later, I realize how prophetic my father's advice was.

So it happened that I began working with Shamnath, as his apprentice.

Shamnath Tickoo's chemist shop was situated on the road that ran along the banks of the Jhelum. Though he was just a regular medical practitioner, he was very popular among the people of old Srinagar. During those days, there was a dearth of doctors, and people would usually go to experienced men like Shamnath for treatment. And Shamnath treated them with such expertise, that they would never even think of going to a doctor.

Inside his shop, at the front, was a huge wooden desk on which was placed a thick slab of glass. Underneath the glass slab, Shamnath had placed a few pictures depicting the scenic beauty of Kashmir. Pictures of his family deities hung on the wall behind his desk. Along the other two walls, he had erected wooden shelves on which were placed his medicines—pills in various glass bottles, solutions, syrups, and ointments. Medicine ran in Shamnath Tickoo's blood.

Shamnath would arrive at his shop early in the morning and after he had offered his prayers to his family deities, he'd make a list of medicines that needed to be bought and then tend to his patients.

He would feel their pulses, and ask most of them to show him their tongues. He would ask some of them to lie down on a wooden bench. A muslin sari, probably his wife's, had been hung over a string to act as a curtain. But the sari was so thin that one could see through it. So I would see him bending over his patients, pressing their stomachs and listening to their heartbeat. Then he would pack some pills in a piece of paper and give them to the patient.

Shamnath had a knack for packing pills. He could fold a sheet of paper into a packet that seemed almost impenetrable, like a Mughal fort. I often imagined patients struggling to open their packets, once they reached their homes and needed to take their medicines. But nobody ever complained.

Initially, Shamnath made me supervise the supply of medicines. My duty was to write down the names of medicines that were almost finished. Then, I'd have to remind him repeatedly to order them.

Once he was satisfied with how I handled my job responsibilities, Shamnath urged me to take an interest in the treatment of patients. He made me sit next to him and observe his methods, as he listened to his patients' woes and inspected their tongues.

'Remember, Prithvi, a clear tongue is an indication of good health. A tongue that looks like a drought-ridden piece of land means trouble. It means, more often than not, troubles of the stomach and liver. So the key to an accurate diagnosis is to check the state of the patient's tongue. If you have learnt this, rest assured, you are halfway to being a doctor.'

Within a few weeks, I had learnt the names of almost all the medicines Shamnath prescribed to his patients. I even began prescribing them myself, when he was absent from his shop.

Shamnath kept his shop closed on Fridays. So each Friday, I would board an early morning bus to Sopore. I would return on Saturday evening and resume my duties Sunday morning. Though Shamnath never said anything to me directly, I learnt from my sisters that in my absence he would visit our home, and speak to my father about my weekly ritual.

During one visit to Sopore, my plastic slippers broke, and I had to return barefooted to Srinagar. When I reached home, I asked my father for some money to buy new slippers, but he said he could not spare any. That night, as I lay awake in the darkness, I decided to ask Shamnath for some money. Throughout the night, I thought of various ways to ask Shamnath to loosen his purse. By the time I'd decided on a way, dawn had broken.

That morning, I went to the shop barefoot. For the next hour or so, I made every possible attempt to get him to notice my bare feet. I climbed on a stool pretending to clean the shelves. I pretended to do some stretching exercises where I touched my feet with my hands. But no matter what I did, Shamnath seemed to remain oblivious to my misery.

No patient had turned up since the morning, and Shamnath sat on his chair, shooing away the mongrel dogs that attempted to relieve themselves at the base of the stone steps leading to his shop. When not shooing away the dogs, he fanned himself with a towel, singing songs of longing penned by a Kashmiri poet. Finally, I lost my patience.

'*Mahra*, I need to tell you something,' I said, using the standard Kashmiri way to address him.

Shamnath stopped fanning himself, and looked at me.

I looked at him rather hesitantly, and then continued, 'In fact, I want to ask you something. Are you happy with my performance?' Before he could answer, I continued, 'If you are satisfied and I am sure you are—I have given you no chance to be unhappy—then please give me some money. Please pay me for my work here.'

I paused in order to gauge his reaction, but there was nothing to read on his face. 'I have never asked for money from you, so far, and I did not intend to, even now, but a great misery has befallen me,' I said, as I looked at my feet. I saw Shamnath's eyes following mine.

Finally, he said what I'd been waiting to hear since the morning.

'Where are your slippers, Prithvi?' he asked.

I had been waiting for this cue, and told him my story.

After I finished, he smiled. He rose from his chair, came up to me, took out some money and put it in my pocket.

I did not check it immediately. But, later in the evening, I took out the money. Shamnath had given me twenty rupees. I rushed barefoot to Lal Chowk, and immediately bought myself a pair of leather sandals. They cost me seventeen rupees. For days, I loved to just walk, so I could show off my sandals to friends, and anyone else who cared to see them.

I worked with Shamnath for close to two years. During this time, I developed a deep understanding of medicine.

A few ripples in the waters of the Jhelum decided my next course of action.

One afternoon, not feeling well, I left the shop early to go home. On the way, while crossing the bridge, I felt slightly dizzy, and sat for a while on the stone steps leading to the river. Boatmen went from one bank of the Jhelum to another, carrying green vegetables, flowers, lotus stems and water chestnuts. There were a few pebbles near me, and I threw them in the river.

As the ripples made by my tossed pebbles spread through the water, it dawned upon me that I could lead a life practising medicine elsewhere, far away from the hustle and bustle of Srinagar. I thought of poplar trees, and apple trees laden with fruit. I thought of gurgling streams, and the scent of the earth. The thought of my own small dispensary amidst such scenes felt like heaven to me. I got up and quickly walked back home.

That evening, I told my father about my plans.

'Have you told Shamnath Tickoo about it?' he asked.

'Well no, it just occurred to me while coming back from his shop this afternoon. I have learnt a lot and I think I can start my own practice now,' I replied.

We sat on rags near the hearth for warmth, while Mother made preparations for our dinner.

'I have been trying hard to get you a government job. One of my acquaintances, Bhan, is very influential. He tells me that a few teaching positions are about to be created in government schools. He has not assured me of anything, but he has said that he will try his best. So until that happens, why don't you just keep working with Shamnath? I am sure you can still learn a lot from him,' Father said. Mother served us our dinner.

I put a morsel of food in my mouth. After I had eaten it, I replied, 'I am not averse to the idea of taking a government job, but right now there is no guarantee that I will get one. Working with Shamnath is also not a bad idea, but, Father, one needs to move on in life. If I work independently, I will be able to contribute in a major way to the family earnings, and then you won't have to work so hard.'

And so, in a month's time I moved to a remote village and established my small dispensary there. As a parting gift, Shamnath gave me many jars of pills. I practised for a few months before Father sent Totha one day to tell me that my job had been arranged. I was to join the Baramulla government school as a teacher.

Time passed by. Much water flowed down the Jhelum. I moved from Baramulla, then moved back. At Ganpatyar, I met Mohini, who would become my wife. Gradually, we rebuilt our lives. We bought a piece of land in a Srinagar suburb. Ravi was born and then we were blessed with a daughter. Father passed away, and then mother, and then Totha left us, too. I worked hard to support my family. The children grew up and I thought that overall our destiny had been benevolent towards us.

I had so many hopes for Ravi. He was such a good son. I remember once, after he was engaged, he was to meet Asha. Not knowing this, I engaged him in a long discussion. But the good son that he was, he did not cut me short. It was only once I had finished that he told me that he had to meet his fiancée. And I was so furious with him, I pushed him out of the house.

In 2009, Ravi's mother passed away as well. She had been missing Ravi too much. Ravi's father still visits us. He is still possessed by that restlessness. There are so many incidents in his story that he told and retold me. Many times, he would remember his son and many episodes from his life. But I won't forget what he told me once when the two of us were alone. We got talking about

Ravi. 'Death is inevitable,' he said. 'But there is one thought that won't let me be at peace—what must he have thought of when he fell to the bullets, all alone?'

The tribal raid of 1947 destroyed many lives. At Bandipore, a group of tribesmen entered the house of Sansar Chand Sadhu at the behest of a local man who bore a grudge against him. Sadhu ran a business of dry fruits in Gilgit and Skardu. On the evening of November 3, 1947, as the family was celebrating the birthday of Sadhu's grandson, the tribesmen, led by this man, barged in. Sadhu's daughter-in-law was holding her son, the birthday boy. The leader of the tribesmen asked her to read the Kalma and marry him. Not only did she refuse, she told the tribesman in chaste Urdu that he was daydreaming. This infuriated him and he shot her, killing her instantly. Then they lined up everyone else and shot them. In all, nine of the Sadhu family were killed that day. Miraculously, the little boy survived. The man had taken his revenge but he was still not satisfied. While leaving, he trampled Sansar Chand's dead body.

At Langate in Kupwara district, Amar Chand Kachroo was told that the tribal invaders were close and that he should flee. He refused. Somehow, he believed that the invaders did not possess firearms. So he asked his family members and some others who had taken refuge in his house to store stones in the attic. Then he closed all the doors. When the tribesmen came, they were showered with stones and slabs of rock salt. They opened fire, killing Amar Chand and his brother. When one of the neighbours later entered their house, he found a dog licking blood in the compound of the house. It had been dripping from the corpse of Amar Chand's brother who was shot in the attic.

In Kupwara, Gushi was the last border village and it was also from where people began their annual pilgrimage to the Sharda temple in the Neelam valley, travelling through Muzaffarabad. Here, the tribal invaders killed many Pandits.

Those who survived in Muzaffarabad witnessed brutalities that would leave them scarred for life. Bishambar Nath Sapru, a resident of Srinagar, was twenty-nine years old when he completed his bachelor's degree in Education. In July 1947, three months before the tribal raid, he was posted to the government high school in Muzaffarabad. Many Kashmiri Pandits were posted in Muzaffarabad at that time. They included the school headmaster, Sham Lal Labroo; the art teacher Kashi Nath Jalali; Sukhdev Kaul, who ran a medical shop; and Shamboo Nath Thalchoor, the sanitary inspector.

In Muzaffarabad, the young Sapru, who had recently married, rented a room on the first floor of a house. On the night of October 21, Sapru was awoken by the sound of something hitting the tin roof of his house. He was paralysed with fear. Earlier in the day, Prithvi Nath Mazari, a schoolteacher posted at Danakcheli, twenty kilometres from Muzaffarabad, had rushed to Muzaffarabad and told the Dogra administrators that he had seen a group of armed tribal invaders. The administrators dismissed his report as a lie and he was punished for 'spreading panic' by being tied to a tree for a few hours.

A few minutes later, two bullets hit the window of Sapru's room. Then a noise erupted in the street below. 'Run to Gopal Chowk,' someone shouted.

When Sapru reached the square, he saw that about three thousand Kashmiri Pandits and Sikhs had already assembled there. There was the sound of gunfire all around. The whole night, the crowd stayed in the square. In the morning, the firing stopped. But one row of houses near the square caught fire, forcing the crowd to flee for safety.

Sapru hid in a deserted house and waited there. An hour or so later, he heard someone shouting in the street—

'You are our brothers now, you have accepted Pakistan.'

He came out and saw a group of tribal invaders. They were armed with rifles and they wore belts of bullets across their shoulders and around their waists. Upon spotting Sapru, one of them pushed him into a crowd of people comprising Pandits and Sikhs. The raider put a piece of green cloth around Sapru's neck and asked him to say '*Pakistan zindabad*'. By this time, the crowd had swelled to ten thousand. More than a hundred armed tribesmen had surrounded them and were herding them along.

In the crowd, Sapru saw his colleague, the art teacher Kashi Nath Jalali. He was extremely unwell and came up to Sapru. 'I cannot walk any further; my knees have given up. I want to leave,' he whispered. But Sapru urged him to keep going since any attempt to leave would anger the raiders. But after a while, Jalali gave up. He tried running away but one of the raiders shot him dead.

Sapru kept walking, but after a while, he looked around. Nobody was watching him. He began walking slowly towards the edge of the crowd and then just took off. He felt something hit his back. A raider had shot at him, but luckily he was out of range. The bullet had hit his coat but had not penetrated. He looked behind—the raider was chasing him. Sapru spotted a big house with its door open. He ran inside and hid. The raider followed him, but could not locate him.

Sapru remained in hiding for some time. Then he decided to look around the house. Maybe there are ladies in the house and they will take pity on me, he thought to himself. On the first floor he came upon seven Kashmiri Muslims seated in a room, eating. Sapru recognized two of them. One of them had studied with him in college and hailed from Baramulla. Sapru had met him on many occasions in Muzaffarabad, and every time his friend had embraced him. The other person he knew was with the police.

On spotting his friend among the group, Sapru felt relieved and walked up to him. 'The raiders almost killed me,' he said.

But the man started hurling abuses at him.

'Oh, you probably don't recognize me; I am Sapru,' he said.

'You have sucked our blood,' the man replied.

The man dragged Sapru outside and began kicking him brutally with his army boots. Sapru lost consciousness. Presuming him to be dead, the group left. It was hours later that Sapru regained consciousness. There was no one in the house now. Sapru weighed his options. If he ventured out, he would definitely be spotted by the invaders and killed. So Sapru dragged himself to the attic and hid there. Through a small window in the room, he had a good view of the bridge across the Kishanganga River.

From that window, Sapru saw the procession from which he had slipped away reach the bridge. The men among the Sikhs were segregated, shot and then pushed into the river. The women were bundled into buses—Sapru counted more than thirty buses—and taken away. In some cases, children were snatched from their arms and thrown on the road.

Sapru also saw many women jumping to their deaths from that bridge, to save their honour.

Later that day, he heard footsteps approaching the attic. Sapru got very scared. A man entered, but he did not look like a raider. He turned out to be the servant of the house's owner. His name was Kalu Khan. Sapru begged him to save his life. Kalu Khan had worked at a Pandit's house in Srinagar, where he had been well treated. He promised to help Sapru. He told him that the raiders had come from Waziristan and other areas, and that some Kashmiris, like those who had been in the house earlier, were acting as their guides. Kalu told Sapru that the owner of the house already knew about the attack and had sent his family to Peshawar. Out of compassion Kalu brought him some food and a little tobacco.

Sapru spent ten days in the attic. From the window he watched the raiders round up Sikhs, shoot them on the bridge and throw their bodies into the river below. Sapru did not venture out at all. He would even relieve himself in the attic and throw his excreta out from the window in the darkness of the night. Often, he heard noises coming from the house below. Men camped there all the time and they slaughtered cattle robbed from those who had been killed or had fled.

Ten days later, Kalu told him of a house where fifty-six Pandits were hiding. The house belonged to a lawyer who had been killed along with his daughter-in-law. With Kalu's help, Sapru was able to shift there.

One night a few men appeared at their doorstep and asked for the headmaster, Sham Nath Labroo. He muttered god's name as they took him away. Everyone thought he would be killed. But he returned after a while. The men only needed a certificate from him for one among them who had been selected for a job in the forest department. He had asked Labroo to issue him a certificate stating that he had passed his matriculation examination with a first division.

After a few days, the invaders rounded up all the Pandits in the house and put them in a prison. One day, a few invaders asked Sapru to hand over all his money. He said he had nothing. They then asked him to part with his shirt and pants. Before leaving, they dragged in six women and raped them in front of Sapru. The captive Pandits spent seventy days like this, watching women being raped and men killed in front of their eyes.

The assistant commissioner of Muzaffarabad, Kacho Ali Mohammed, who later became a minister in the Jammu and Kashmir government, saved the lives of many Pandits during those days. He gave shelter to a few women to save them from the clutches of the tribesmen.

Sapru and others had lost hope of reuniting with their families. Now the question was that of survival. Sapru got a job at a Muslim bakery where his task was to prepare dough. The owner gave him an old shirt to wear. But after two days he was asked to leave since the baker's clients were objecting to an 'infidel' preparing dough for their bread.

Many Pandits had converted to Islam to save their lives. After losing his job, Sapru approached a man who taught Arabic at his school. In the presence of fifteen men, a maulvi converted Bishambar Nath Sapru to Ghulam Mohammed. After his conversion, he was served some rice and sweetmeats, and someone blew a bugle to welcome him into his new faith.

After four months of living in hell, Sapru and a few others planned to escape. They managed to get some warm clothing, and, posing as Kashmiri salt merchants, crossed over to Indian-administered Kashmir. It was then that he was reunited with his family.

There had been mass conversions during the tribal raid. At several places, the invaders had herded Pandits to a ground where, like their ancestors from Afghanistan who ruled Kashmir once, they slaughtered a calf, cooked it and forced the

Pandits to eat it, and then read the Kalma while cutting their sacred thread.

Conservative estimates suggest that thousands were converted forcibly to Islam. Most of them were later reconverted to Hinduism through the efforts of Pandit saints like Swami Nand Lal and social reformers like Tara Chand (Kashyap Bandhu). Totha said he had seen one such ceremony in Goiteng, Kupwara, where Swami Nand Lal tied the sacred thread across the shoulders of hundreds of men. To save them from the ignominy of any future discrimination by their fellow Brahmins, the swami had asked one of his followers to cook some turmeric rice. Then, everyone was asked to eat a little from the huge plate. The remaining rice was eaten by the swami himself to demonstrate that all of them were equals.

A few in Sopore and elsewhere refused to reconvert to Hinduism. They had lost all hope. 'What if the savages come back?' they asked.

PART FIVE

The restlessness that Ravi's father suffered affected Ma as well. Some afternoons, Father would be taking a nap and suddenly Ma would wake him up. 'I think I will go to Jammu,' she would say. 'But we don't have a reservation; we could have booked a train ticket or something,' Father would say. 'No, I will go in a bus.' And she would pack a small bag and just leave. From Jammu, Father's brother would call and complain about how Ma had refused to eat lunch, or stay overnight. 'She just came on a flying visit; after much insisting she accepted a cup of tea,' he would say.

In the summer of 2004, Ma began to experience unexpected falls while she went out on walks or to do the shopping. At first we thought it was the result of her old back problem. But within a few weeks, the falls became far too frequent and during one such episode she was hurt badly. She also began to complain that her voice was turning hoarse. We dismissed her fears initially, but soon even we began to notice the changes. Within weeks she developed an acute slur in her speech.

Like most Kashmiris of previous generations, my parents had very little faith in doctors in Delhi. Whenever an illness arose, the conversation inevitably veered towards the prowess of Kashmiri doctors like Ali Jan, or Naseer, or Shunglu. So father took Ma to Jammu where a family friend had arranged an out-of-turn appointment with the famous Kashmiri neurologist, Dr Sushil Razdan. He was like a demigod for many Kashmiris. From Kashmir Valley, hordes of people, now bearing the trauma of violence, visited him for treatment. After examining Ma,

Dr Razdan looked at my father and said—I have bad news. Ma, he told us, was suffering from a rare neurological disorder called motor neurone disease. She would lose her voice completely, and soon she would be restricted to bed. Her muscles would weaken one by one and then she would even lose her ability to swallow food.

The news was shattering. Dr Razdan's words began to come true within the next few months. Ma lost her power of speech. Then it became too difficult for her to walk. Ultimately, she took to her bed. She would be in acute pain at times. She also began to have severe emotional outbursts, especially prolonged episodes of crying. She couldn't accept what had happened to her. There was not a single neurologist in the country whose advice I did not seek. When her body contorted with pain and her face turned red, Ma sometimes looked at me with hope, as if I could conjure up a miracle. This helplessness made me very angry. I felt like putting the gods through her pain—putting them into a hat, reciting some magic words and turning them into rabbits, their veins throbbing violently, like Ma's. As saliva dripped from her mouth and she struggled hard to swallow mashed bottle gourd, I remembered the taste of the meals cooked by her.

But even though she was completely incapacitated, her mental faculties became sharper than ever. She would hear a knock at the door before Father or I did. She knew when the television was running on the inverter battery. Only she remembered death anniversaries, and it was she who would alert Father, as he reached for his Marie biscuit in the morning, that he was supposed to fast that day.

After she developed this condition, I thought it was imperative that we at least have a house of our own. So I booked a flat in a Delhi suburb and I took Father to have a look.

'But where will so much money come from?' he asked.

I told him that I had applied for a loan. He looked at me in disbelief. Led by the builder's manager, we went inside the flat. Father moved from one room to another; he looked at the ceilings. I was disappointed, since he didn't say anything.

'Do you like it?' I asked.

'Yes, it is nice,' he replied.

Two days later, I paid the booking amount to the builder. The same day, my loan was sanctioned as well. I came home and shared the news with my father.

'Are you serious about buying this house?' he asked. 'How will you repay the loan? Where will so much money come from?' I explained to him that every month a fixed amount would be deducted from my bank account. He kept silent for a while. 'I want to see it again,' he said, finally.

'Why? Didn't you see it the other day?'

'No, I remember nothing. I never thought you would actually book it.'

I took him there again the next day. This time he checked everything thoroughly. The first thing he did, of course, was to turn on the tap. 'Oh,' he smiled, 'running water.'

A few months later, we shifted house. On a wheelchair, I gave Ma a tour of the entire house. When we entered the kitchen, she was overcome with emotion. She cried a lot.

We have been in exile for more than two decades. Kashmir is a memory, an overdose of nostalgia. But beyond this, there is nothing. Many among us have moved on. For most of us, Kashmir means a calendar hanging in our parents' bedroom, or a mutton dish cooked in the traditional way on Shivratri, or a cousin's marriage that the elders insist must be solemnized in Jammu.

A few of my friends, who live in a Delhi suburb, try and meet on weekends, and indulge in nightlong revelries of food and drink, and the singing of Kashmiri songs. They are all top corporate executives, and live in plush apartments. Some of them are too young to remember anything of Kashmir. But for some, these songs bring a rush of memory. One among these friends calls me at times from Moscow, where he frequently goes on business trips. After deals have been clinched he gets drunk 'outside Kremlin', as he insists when he calls. 'I just wanted to talk to someone in Kashmiri,' he says. We talk about the old days, crack jokes that only a Kashmiri can understand, and sometimes, he gets emotional as a result and cries.

My friend has a young daughter who started going to school recently. He would often tell her stories about Kashmir, and how they had a home there, but it had been burnt down. A few months into school, the little girl's teacher called her parents. 'Your daughter seems to have a psychological problem,' she told them. She said they had been doing a class exercise in which everyone was supposed to say a few lines about their home. When her turn came, the girl said she had no home. When pressed further, she said her family had a house but it had been burnt down. The parents apologized and explained why their daughter had said what she did. Later they made sure to tell their daughter that the flat they now lived in was indeed their home.

Over the last few years, I have often thought about exile, and about the displaced Pandit families, especially those living in big cities like Delhi. I began to worry that the story of our community would be lost in the next few decades. It was only because of the previous generation that our customs and traditions were being kept alive. It is people from my father's generation who know how to consult an almanac and keep track of festivals and the death anniversaries of ancestors. They created mini Kashmirs wherever they settled. But after them, there will be nobody left to remember. We are losing our tradition, our links to the place where we came from. This is evident during weddings, or when someone dies. Tradition is like an embarrassing grandparent who needs to be fed and put back to bed in a back room.

My uncle died recently—the one who was a movie buff. He had been unwell for months and passed away in his sleep in his daughter's house in Delhi. We tried hard to get hold of a priest who knew the proper Kashmiri rituals. But we couldn't find anybody. Finally we decided to engage a local priest at the cremation ground. As my uncle was being prepared for his final journey, an old man came and whispered that the departed should lie with his head facing the east. We quickly did that. Everyone was silent. We recited whatever prayers we could and then carried him away to the cremation ground. I returned home late that night. I was devastated. At least the dead merit dignity; their farewell ought to be performed in the same manner as that of their forefathers. I remembered all those cycle rides he took me on. I remembered the family jokes around him. I remembered how he had insisted on carrying sacks of rice over his back during my sister's wedding.

I took a bath and sat silently in my father's *thokur kuth*, and I recited the *Durgasaptashati*. Dear Uncle, may you find eternal peace! May you never be rendered homeless again!

Over the past decade I have visited Kashmir regularly as a journalist. I have reported on damning episodes of human rights violations by security personnel; I have reported on the dreaded knock on the door in the middle of the night; I have reported on young women whose husbands have disappeared, making them 'half widows'; I have reported on young boys for whom death has become a spectacle. But in all these years I had never gathered the courage to visit my home in Srinagar. In fact, I would even avoid travelling in that general direction. But over the last few years, the urge became more powerful, as if it were my compulsory pilgrimage to Mecca. As if some umbilical cord with memory would be severed if I did not visit.

During my reporting assignments I had met Ali Mohammed, an elderly Kashmiri driver. Over several assignments we grew fond of each other. He reminded me of Totha. Travelling with him across Kashmir and listening to his stories on long journeys were like taking a walk through Kashmir's history. He had so many stories to share of the old times. He spoke fondly of how his Pandit teacher would box his ears because he couldn't learn a certain lesson; or how he drove the car of the legendary Pandit doctor Jagat Mohini who ran the Ratan Rani hospital right up to her death in 2009; or how he skipped meals at his house to eat at a Pandit's house because he liked their preparation of collard greens.

'I wouldn't take any nonsense from anyone,' he said. 'But now one has to control one's temper. The boys have guns now, and they will show no consideration towards the wrinkles on my face.' Ali Mohammed—most youngsters called him Chacha— lamented the loss of what we once had in Kashmir. 'The old days are gone,' he often said, as we sat in his car, sharing cigarettes and our love for the singer Kailash Mehra.

Whenever I went to Kashmir, I always made it a point to visit the Kshir Bhawani temple. There, I felt connected to my ancestors. A day before, I would tell chacha about my plans. He would arrive early the next morning, and together we would drive to the temple. 'It is important to be in touch with one's roots,' he would tell me. We never discussed money—he would accept whatever I put in his shirt pocket. On many afternoons, he would park the car outside Ahdoo's restaurant and we would sit like old friends, sharing a quintessential Kashmiri meal of rice, roganjosh and collard greens.

When going back home became inevitable in my mind, I told chacha about it. *Aaesh karith*—with pleasure, he said like always. Two journalist friends, Suhail and Zubair, also accompanied me. 'Are you sure you want to do this?' Suhail asked when I shared my decision with him. It would be a painful experience, he knew. Two years ago, a massive earthquake had almost brought down his house, and for days afterwards he would speak of nothing else but the cracks that had developed in his house. How could I explain my decision to him, I thought. 'I need to click pictures, Suhail,' I said finally. 'For my mother.'

So on the morning of a day in September 2007, the three of us sat in Chacha's Tavera and my journey towards home began. From Lal Chowk, it took us a few minutes to cross the Ram Bagh bridge, and from there we drove on to Natipora. Until then I was all right. But soon afterwards, my heart began to sink. I hoped it did not show on my face.

Initially, I missed the turn-off for our house. That was the spot where the school bus would drop us, and we would walk the rest of the way home. But now everything had changed. The road had become congested. New shops and houses had come up all over the place. It was only when we reached the last bus

stop on the road that I realized where we were, and asked
Chacha to make a U-turn. Soon, I saw the deserted temple on
my right. A little further ahead, the gurudwara.

*I am now standing at one end of my street, my locality. On my left,
Rehman the milkman's shop is closed. Is he alive, or has the monster
of violence consumed him as well? It is 3 p.m. and there is nobody
outside. I walk ahead. Suhail and Zubair follow me. My house
should be somewhere here. Yes, yes, it is. On my left. I turn. It is in
front of me. The huge blue gate is still there. The name* Aabshar—
*waterfall—is still painted on a small board. The apple tree used to
be visible from the street. Wait . . . where is it? It is not there. Is this
my house?*

A man walks up to me. 'Are you looking for someone?'
he asks.

I look at him. 'I used to live here long ago,' I mutter.

'Oh!' he says; his face softens. He takes a step forward and
hugs me. 'I stay in that house,' he points to a house. 'My name is
Gazanfar Ali; I am an advocate.'

'It belonged to the Razdans?' I ask.

'Yes.'

Then I am standing right in front of my house.

'This is your home as well. Come inside, have some tea.'

I want to go inside my house, my home, my only home.

'Who lives here now?' I ask him.

'I don't know much about them; the man stays with his wife
and her parents. He won't be there, but his father-in-law is
always at home,' he says. 'The Razdans came here a few years
ago. Mr Razdan had requested me to search for a small velvet
purse that had belonged to his father. Luckily I found it and
handed it over to him.'

I look at Zubair and Suhail. They watch this silently as if

from the sidelines of a film set. 'Stop by at my place once you've visited your home,' Ali says.

We enter through the gate.

The lawn is just like we had left it, except that the grass has worn away. The small fence still runs around it, but it is broken at many places. The apple tree is no longer there. It was probably cut down.

'Will you knock at the door?' I ask Suhail. Two gentle knocks. A man appears at the door. *Wanyu*, he says. Tell me? I don't know what to say to him.

Zubair clears his throat. 'Actually, he used to live here long ago,' he looks at me.

The man stares at me; he doesn't know how to process this information. 'Come inside,' he gives up finally.

I steal a glance towards the top right-hand side of the door. The fish-shaped doorbell is still there. But it is not functional now. I can see the wire protruding from its belly. I still haven't looked towards my right, towards what used to be our kitchen garden, beyond which used to be Ravi's kitchen garden, and then his home.

I am led inside, to our living room. An elderly woman—she is the man's wife—is lying on a carpet. She gets up, embarrassed, adjusting her head scarf. She looks at her husband. She is smiling a particular smile, which in Kashmir one does when one cannot ask a question but nevertheless expects an answer. 'They used to live here,' he tells her. Suddenly I realize Zubair and Suhail are not with me. Where are they? 'One minute, please, I'll just go and see where my friends are!' I say as I leave the room. It is probably a good thing to do, as it will give them some time to discuss me. I open the front door. I find Zubair and Suhail outside. Suhail's back is towards me, but I understand.

He is weeping helplessly, at the thought of a man knocking at his own door, finding someone else opening it, and then seeking permission to enter his own house. I hold his hands; we embrace. It takes him a few minutes to compose himself. I lead them inside.

We sit on chairs. The woman is looking at me. I don't know why, but I think she is hard of hearing. I JUST CAME TO TAKE A LOOK. IT'S BEEN A LONG TIME SINCE WE LIVED HERE. WE LIVE IN DELHI NOW. WE HAVE OUR OWN HOUSE. WE ARE SETTLED THERE (Yes, settled!) I JUST WANT TO CLICK A FEW PICTURES AND SHOW THEM TO MY PARENTS. THEY HAVEN'T BEEN ABLE TO RETURN SINCE 1990.

Her smile changes. It's a different smile now. It is devoid of that question mark. It's a smile of relief. YES, DON'T WORRY, I KNOW HOW IT FEELS—THE THOUGHT OF SOMEONE COMING AND CLAIMING YOUR HOUSE. IT IS YOUR HOUSE NOW. I HAVE JUST COME TO PLACE IT IN MY MEMORY.

Tea arrives. We drink it silently. There are a few questions about what I do and where I live. But my mind is elsewhere. I remember there used to be a cupboard behind where I sit now, with glass doors. We used to call it the 'showpiece almari'. It held small decorative items—six small clay statues of a military band, photo frames, a dancing girl who gyrated gracefully when nudged, a wire cycle, a big star filled with blue gel. None of it is there now.

'The house was in very bad condition,' the man says. 'When we shifted the walls were crumbling; we had to spend a lot of money on renovation.'

Sir, quote a price and I will buy it from you right away. Bad condition! Do you, sir, even realize what it means for me to be sitting in this house? This house built with my father's Provident Fund savings and my mother's bridal jewellery; this house where my mother sat on her haunches and mopped the long, red-cemented corridor each morning; the house we left forever to become refugees and court suffering and homelessness.

Every memory comes back to me. The boys who had assembled on the street below on that cold evening in 1990, distributing our houses among themselves; that taxi ride to Jammu and that man showing us his fist and wishing us death; truck after truck of refugees under that tarpaulin, that woman's blank eyes; the heat and other horrors of those one-room dwellings; mother's tears and that young man holding the remains of a wedding feast on a plate outside our room; the humiliation of a door-less toilet; the ignominy of suffering landlords.

And you, sir, say this house was in bad condition! Do you know the comfort of lying under quilts in the room adjacent to where we are sitting now? Do you know the touch of the breeze that flows by when you are reading in the room upstairs, watching the apple-laden tree swaying gently? Or the joy of watching those blooming roses in the lawn? Or enjoying the sun on the rear balcony?

And sir, the house was in bad condition because those who looted our belongings also ripped off the taps and the water seeped in everywhere.

The tea is finished. Can we go upstairs, please? I climb the stairs. Can we go into that room? The shelf where we used to keep our books—there are no books. The shelf is filled with onions and garlic. Oh, how it breaks my heart! From the window I look out onto the kitchen garden. There is no kitchen garden— there is no mountain mint, there are no rose shrubs. Ravi's house stands silently. A motorcycle is parked in the front, just like his used to be. But it belongs to the new occupants of the house. I feel like opening the window and whistling the way Ma used to when she wanted to speak to her brother, or mother. I imagine Ravi will peep out from the window and sing that ditty to me teasingly—*Vicky ko bhar do dickey mein, apna kaam karega.*

I click pictures furiously. The BSF camp is no longer behind the house. Their campus is now a forest of unkempt grass and wild bushes; some houses have been built there as well. The rear wooden balcony has collapsed. I am still thinking about our books. What happened to them? Were they sold to a scrap dealer, or were their bindings ripped off and their pages torn into shreds in some frenzy?

The man is getting a bit restless now. He is done showing me around what happens to be his house now. I still want to go to the attic and check if something is left of my huge collection of comics and Enid Blyton series, many of which I won by collecting lucky coupons from packs of Double Yum chewing gum. There is also the 'best deodar wood' that Father had procured just before we had to leave. For years he lamented over how that wood had been left back home.

I step out. I climb down the wooden stairs and hold the baluster for a moment. I want to retain the memory of its feel. I sit on my veranda and tie my shoelaces. The water works board stating our connection number is still there: 44732. A piece of driftwood a cousin had lovingly mounted on the wall is there as well. The looters would have thought nothing of it. I shake hands with the man. I look at the spot where the apple tree used to be. I remember how Dedda used to sit there, or how Totha would take me there and try and keep me busy playing with pebbles. I'm reminded of one Sunday evening when a cousin and I were watching television and lightning struck suddenly. It struck a tree near the mosque and then passed through our antenna and we watched in fear as burning debris fell into the BSF camp. Ma was so angry that we had switched on the television set in that dreadful storm, against her advice. For days, we couldn't watch television since the antenna could not be replaced immediately.

'There used to be an apple tree there,' I point with my finger.

'Oh, we got it cut; it was occupying too much space.'

Ghulam Hasan Sofi's voice rings in my ears—

B'e thavnus chaetit'h tabardaaran
Yaaro wun baalyaaro wun
Chh'e kamyu karenai taavei'z pun?

I was split apart by the woodcutter
My friend, my beloved, tell me:
who has cast a spell on you?

In *The Murderers Are Among Us*, Simon Wiesenthal writes— 'However this war may end, we have won the war against you; none of you will be left to bear witness, but even if someone were to survive, the world would not believe him.'

Over the years, the narrative of what led to the exodus of the Kashmiri Pandits from the Valley has been changed. A series of untruths have been spoken so many times that they have almost become the truth. One major untruth is that the Pandits were made to leave Kashmir under a government design to discredit the Kashmiri secessionist movement. One of the scapegoats chosen for this untruth was the former governor of the state, Jagmohan.

'The Pandits were encouraged by Jagmohan to leave so that he could deal with us firmly.' One kept hearing this. Initially, I didn't care. But now I seethe with anger whenever I come across this propaganda. I have become determined—to paraphrase Agha Shahid Ali—that my memory must come in the way of this untrue history. Another problem is the apathy of the media and a majority of India's intellectual class who refuse to even acknowledge the suffering of the Pandits. No campaigns were ever run for us; no fellowships or grants given for research on our exodus. For the media, the Kashmir issue has remained largely black and white—here are a people who were victims of brutalization at the hands of the Indian state. But the media has failed to see, and has largely ignored the fact that the same people also victimized another people.

It has become unfashionable to speak about us, or raise the issue of our exodus. But I have made it my mission to talk about the 'other story' of Kashmir. Like the tramp in Naipaul's *In a Free State*, I have reduced my life to names and numbers. I have memorized the name of every Pandit killed during those dark days, and the circumstances in which he or she was killed. I have memorized the number of people killed in each district. I have memorized how many of us were registered as refugees in Jammu and elsewhere.

Another untruth that leaves me fuming is the assertion that nobody touched the handful of Pandit families that had chosen to remain in the Valley. In a *Paris Review* interview, holocaust survivor and acclaimed writer Primo Levi is asked, 'Are they still strongly anti-Semitic in Poland today?' 'They're not any more. For lack of material!' he replies. That is roughly what happened in Kashmir as well. Some of us would return once a year to celebrate a festival at Kshir Bhawani and murderers like

Bitta Karate, who nurse political ambitions now, would visit and hug elderly women and pictures would be taken and published prominently in local newspapers.

While I know there are many among the Kashmiri Muslims who want us back, I am also aware of what happened to some of us who chose to stay back. That is why meeting Vinod Dhar was very important.

It is very difficult to get Vinod Dhar on the telephone. The first time I call him, he picks up the phone after the first ring. It is evening, and there is absolute silence on the other end for a few seconds before I hear two 'hellos' in quick succession, the second more impatient than the first.

I speak to him in Hindi. For months, I've been struggling to get in touch with people whose family members were killed by militants, to record their stories. The problem is that no one really says 'no'. But everyone is evasive.

'Yes, yes, come over any time. We will have lunch. My home is your home, after all.'

'Any time' is the problem. So I take a deep breath.

'So when can I come?'

Same response. 'Any time.'

'How about tomorrow morning?'

'Ah, well, the thing is, there is a wedding in the family. So we won't be here tomorrow. You know this is wedding season.'

'Ok, so when then?'

'Give me a call on Monday. We will surely meet then.'

On Monday I call. There is no response. I call again on Tuesday. The phone is answered.

'Hello, hellooooo, yes, who do you want to speak to . . . Oh, yes, yes, how are you? Yes, we are back. Let me call you this evening, and then we can meet.'

The call is never returned. The next morning I call again. The phone is not answered. I try five times. Ten times. No response.

Those who agree to meet are keen to talk about their mastery of the history of Kashmir. 'You see, according to Nilmat Purana . . .'

Out of respect, I listen to them for a while.

'Sir, I was asking you about 1990 . . .'

'Your tea is getting cold. Here, have a biscuit. You will stay for lunch, won't you?'

'Sir . . . 1990?'

'When are you here next? We can sit at ease next time and have a long chat.'

'But, sir, I heard about Nilmat Purana for thirty minutes . . .'

But the conversation is over by that time. One more biscuit, one more conversation about lunch and you want to escape badly. Dead end.

With Vinod Dhar, I know I have to be more persistent.

'Vinod ji, I want to meet you.'

'For what?'

'I'm writing a book and I was hoping to meet you.'

Long silence. 'Hello, Vinod ji, are you there?'

'What will it achieve now, speaking of those days? I am trying to forget it all.'

It sounds as if Vinod Dhar has jumped into a well and speaks to me from there.

You cannot argue with the act of forgetting. Trying to forget. Perhaps I don't understand the importance of forgetting. Perhaps it is important for Vinod Dhar to forget. For someone who lost his entire family in the matter of a few minutes one cold January night, it is important to forget. For someone who is the lone survivor of a massacre that claimed twenty-three members—from his family and extended family and neighbours.

I spoke to him about how I understood why he did not want to talk about it, but how important it was to talk about it. I quoted Milan Kundera: *The struggle of man against power is the struggle of memory against forgetting.*

'Call me tomorrow,' he finally says.

The next morning, Vinod Dhar does not answer his phone. An hour later, I call again. This time it is switched off. Two hours later, someone else answers the phone.

'He is not well,' the man says. That evening I call again. This time Vinod answers.

'Yes, I was not well. You were writing a book, you said. But you see there is no point talking about what happened to me. I'm trying to forget it.'

A part of me wants to give up. Then I remember the images I have seen of the dead the morning after, lined up on dry straw. Men, women, children. And the reports of their Muslim neighbours wailing over the bodies. So I chew on the inside of my cheek till it bleeds, gulp down a stiff drink and say, 'Please Vinod ji, you'll be doing me a great favour if you meet me.'

There is a pause at the other end. And then, 'I don't know what will come of it,' he says.

'Consider it a favour to me,' I say again.

'Hmm . . .' he sighs. 'Ok, call me tomorrow morning at nine.'

At nine the next morning, his phone is switched off.

I am in a hotel. Its walls are damp and the bed sheets reek of lovemaking. I haven't told any of my relatives that I am in Jammu. It would be difficult to work if I stayed with them; it would be impossible to step out without them fussing over breakfast and lunch, and dinner. Also, I know there will be questions about my own homelessness, about why over the past year I've been coming alone to attend family weddings. I have no answers for them. What I can tell them is something they wouldn't understand.

How can I share with them the strong imagery in my mind of a home, of how I failed to set it up in reality.

Back in Delhi, in my bedroom, which used to be 'our' bedroom, there are still closets filled with her clothes, and shoes, her nail paint, her fragrances. She is no longer there.

For my relatives, who worry about my meals and my other comforts, and who want to ask questions, exile is something that they think of while opening up an old family album, or while watching videos of their visit to Kshir Bhawani, shot on their newly acquired Sony Handycams. They are 'settled' in their mind otherwise. Their new houses are their homes. Jammu is their Shahar now. They celebrate birthdays, exam results, new house paint, a new car—everything.

For me, though, exile is permanent. Homelessness is permanent. I am uprooted in my mind. There is nothing I can do about it. My idea of home is too perfect. My idea of love is too perfect. And home and love are too intertwined. I am like my grandfather, who never left his village his whole life. It was deeply embedded in his matrix, too perfect to be replicated elsewhere.

Malcolm Lowry wrote, 'I have no house, only a shadow.'

I have no home, only images. And in those closets in my bedroom, I could only conjure up images of home. And now, that too is gone.

I think Vinod Dhar will not meet me. I am saddened, but I understand. I have come to Jammu to record his story, but since he is playing truant, I have a lot of time. The four walls of the hotel depress me. I look out of the window. An old man is using a net to fish out leaves from the hotel swimming pool. In a banquet hall next to it, preparations are underway for the evening's event. Waiters wearing uniforms soiled with curry stains carry crockery and cartons of alcohol.

I step out. I decide to go to the old city, towards the Rajput Sabha where we had spent a few weeks more than two decades ago. I take an autorickshaw and get off at the Matador stand. I want to walk from here through the bustling bazaar. It is morning and many shops are yet to open. In many ways nothing has changed. Shop owners, who have just opened the shutters of their shops, burn camphor in small steel containers to ward off the evil eye. Two priests wearing their peculiar headgear ring small bells and utter some indecipherable hymn and float from shop to shop, seeking alms. The dye shops are open with workers immersing fabric in their boiling, coloured concoctions.

Images from those few weeks we spent at Rajput Sabha come back to me. From the terrace of the Sabha, I would often stand and watch the world go by through the bazaar. To escape the monotony of our room, I used to spend hours on the roof. But today, I am the world. I look up, almost expecting to see a boy, fourteen years old, watching me, to escape his new life.

I turn left and am now standing in front of the main entrance of the Rajput Sabha. But there are no stairs now. I look up. They are turning it into a shopping complex. There is cement and other construction material everywhere. Banners of cell phone companies offering deals have already come up. I stand there transfixed, and I remember a very hot afternoon. There were hardly any people on the street. When I think of that day, I always see it as a phantasmagoria of sorts. In it, I imagine a shopkeeper sitting on a cushion in front of his desk. He has fallen asleep and his mouth is open and a fly flits in and out of it.

The grill door of the Sabha's main entrance is locked as it always was from lunchtime onwards. And from inside, Vishal comes out and joins me at the entrance. He is wearing a crisp white shirt and trousers and shining moccasins. A sugarcane vendor passes by. He sells sugarcane pieces, kebab-like, chilled under a slab of ice. Vishal passes some money through the grill and buys some sugarcane. We sit on the stairs and chew on the pieces. Vishal was a friend of the Sabha's caretaker. He often visited, along with some of his friends, and they just sat and gossiped and laughed over the cutouts of actresses the caretaker had pasted in his room. It was Vishal who cultivated in me a life-long passion for singing. Sitting on those marble stairs, he would break into a song from a film of the late eighties, *Awaargi*.

Chamakte chand ko toota hua taara bana daala
Meri aawargi ne mujhko aawara bana daala

A shining moon turned into a fallen star
My vagrancy turned me into a vagrant

Somehow, that song stayed with me. It shaped me, moulded me into its meanings; it became my cast. In one stanza, the poet says—

Mein is duniya ko aksar dekh kar hairaan hota hun
Na mujh se ban saka chhota sa ghar, din raat rota hun

I often marvel when I look at the world
I could not even build a small house: day and night I cry

This image is so clear in my mind, and so magnified, that I forget it happened two decades ago. I turn back. Behind me is a small temple and there are two benches in front of it, and a small see-saw for children. Sometimes, memory has a mind of its own. It takes off on autopilot, and flashes small incidents in front of you—incidents one has not remembered for years. Behind the temple is the shopkeeper's house on the stairs of which I would stand and watch *Mahabharat*. I close my eyes and just sit there. An alcoholic is sleeping on the other bench.

I take out my cell phone and I dial Vinod Dhar's number again. The phone rings. On the second ring, the phone is answered.

'Where are you?' Vinod Dhar asks.

I tell him.

'Oh, you are five minutes away. Come to the coffee shop outside the Secretariat. I'll see you there.'

I pick up my bag and start running.

The Secretariat is a depressing building from where the government functions. In Jammu and Kashmir though, there are two Secretariats. In the winters, the Secretariat operates from Jammu. In the summers, it is shifted to Srinagar. This is known as the Durbar Move. At this time the Secretariat is in Jammu and so is Vinod Dhar.

I enter the coffee shop. It is a small place. Behind the counter, in an open space, there are three stone tables with stone benches on either side. Vinod is standing there. I recognize him from a picture I have seen of him in a news report. In it, he sits on a chair, outside his dwelling in the refugee camp, and looks away from the camera. And now, he is shaking hands with me. His hair is short and he hasn't shaved for a few days. He wears a sky-blue shirt. He breaks into a boyish smile and leads me to one of the benches. He sits across the table from me. Then he takes a good look at me. 'I had heard about how journalists can go after someone. Today, I have experienced it with you. I've never met anybody who is as persistent as you,' he says.

Vinod Dhar speaks nervously and he bites his nails as he speaks. And he speaks for the entire time he spends with me. As he speaks, spit accumulates at the corners of his lips.

'You must be thinking I speak all the time,' he says five minutes after we have sat down. 'My psychiatrist says I have aged, but I stopped growing mentally on January 25, 1998.' That is not entirely true though. Vinod is quite mature. He understands what he has gone through. Recognizing the fact that one particular incident in his life has left psychological scars is an act of maturity itself.

Vinod Dhar was fourteen in 1998. His family and his uncles lived in Wandhama, a sleepy hamlet in Kashmir's Gandarbal district. His family and three other Pandit families had thought of leaving like everyone else in 1990, but then decided against it. Their sustenance depended on agriculture, and the family elders were not sure how Jammu would turn out to be for them.

'And then once everyone else left, it became too difficult to leave after that,' says Vinod. In 1992, when they felt threatened, they decided to leave once again.

'We tried selling our properties, but certain elements within the village prohibited others from buying them,' says Vinod. He remembers how they had given up after that.

'My father said Jammu was very costly and we wouldn't be able to survive there,' recalls Vinod.

Shortly afterwards, an army camp was established near their village. It made them feel secure. Life moved on. They tilled their land, bought provisions from neighbouring shops and restricted their religious activities to a small temple near their house.

In 1996, however, the army camp moved. And Vinod recalls how shortly afterwards, armed militants began to be seen in the village. The small group of Pandits always tried to steer clear of both the army and the militants.

On the afternoon of January 25, 1998, Vinod Dhar ventured out after feasting on a lunch prepared by his mother. A meal of rice and turnip and lotus stem curry, he recalls. He went to a nearby field to play cricket with some friends. He returned after sunset. Inside, it was work as usual. His mother was preparing dinner and his father was enjoying a cup of tea. His brother was asleep upstairs. He had just entered when a group of armed men barged into their house. Even in the dim light, their rifles glistened. Vinod's father addressed them. They made themselves comfortable and asked for tea. Vinod's mother rushed to make tea.

After drinking tea, the group went outside. Vinod remembers that one of them carried a wireless set and soon after they left, it began to crackle. After a few minutes, Vinod heard gunshots outside. He rushed to his mother and held her hand. Together, they tried climbing up to the first floor when his mother was shot from behind. His brother, who rushed down after hearing gunshots, was shot as well. Vinod reached upstairs and hid himself behind a heap of cow dung cakes, used as fuel. The group of terrorists shot dead twenty-three people that day. They were shot and then dragged into the main compound of Vinod's house. After killing everyone, some of the terrorists came upstairs. Vinod held his breath. One of them poked his rifle through the dung cakes, narrowly missing Vinod's face.

And then they left. Their mission was accomplished. Vinod stayed where he was.

It was the night of Shab-e-Qadr—'Night of Destiny'— the night of Ramzan when the first verse of the Koran was revealed to the Prophet Mohammed by Jibreel.

After midnight, Vinod slowly came down the stairs. He looked at the bodies that lay outside. It was freezing cold. He looked at them for a few minutes and then went back inside. One by one he dragged out heavy quilts from his house and put them over the bodies. Then he went back and hid behind the cow dung cakes.

In the wee hours of the morning, an army patrol entered Vinod's compound. But he did not venture out, because he had seen the terrorists wearing similar military fatigues. It was only when he saw a police party that he came out and met them.

'My mind was absolutely numb,' he recalls fourteen years later. 'The realization that I had lost my entire family did not dawn upon me at all.'

After the civil administration authorities arrived, the people from the village started pouring in. Vinod remembers the exact words he uttered to the officer in charge upon spotting his Muslim neighbours.

'I told him: "*In mein se koi haraami inhe haath nahi lagayega.*" None of these bastards will touch the bodies.'

We are still sitting in the coffee shop and it is now lunchtime. Many Muslim employees are there as well. There is no vacant spot available, so one of them sits next to me. He is eating a patty. As Vinod says this, he shuffles his feet uneasily. There is a pause. The Muslim walks away.

I remember some of the reports I had read of the massacre. One report described how Muslim women were seen wailing over the dead bodies of Vinod's family members and others.

'I will tell you something,' Vinod says, 'when the gun shots were being fired, the people of the village increased the volume of the loudspeaker in the mosque to muffle the sound of the gunfire.'

Nobody came out of their homes the whole night. They only came out later, after daylight had broken.

'They wanted to shed *magarmacch ke aansu*—crocodile tears,' says Vinod.

All twenty-three pyres were lit by Vinod. Later in the day, the then prime minister, I.K. Gujral, arrived at Vinod's village. Vinod was so young, recalls Sanjay Tickoo, a community leader who was there, that he wanted to take a ride in Gujral's helicopter.

Vinod was later shifted to a BSF camp in Jammu where he completed his schooling and later his graduation in commerce. After he lost his family, Vinod was harassed by his relatives who wanted a share of his ex gratia settlement. 'They would beat me up for money,' he recalls.

Vinod now works as a clerk with the state government. 'I wanted to study more, gain more knowledge. I am pursuing a Master's in History, but I haven't been able to clear it so far.' As proof of his knowledge-seeking, Vinod throws a Bernard Shaw quote at me. 'Where wealth accumulates, men decay.'

Vinod lives in the Jagti refugee settlement for Kashmiri Pandits, outside Jammu city. When he is in Srinagar, does he ever feel like returning to his village? 'I don't go anywhere when I am in Srinagar. I don't want to return to my village. But sometimes I go to the Kshir Bhawani temple and sit in front of the goddess. I used to go there with my mother,' he says.

Vinod is alone. 'Why don't you marry?' I ask him. He is not looking at me, he is lost in thought. 'You know that night, I sat hidden the whole night, I did not cry, I was like a stone.' And then he looks at me; he has heard my question. 'I cannot marry; I'm too insecure. What if she doesn't like me tomorrow and decides to leave me? Then what will I do?'

'I have never been to Delhi, or Bombay. I wonder how it would be to go to Europe. You live in Delhi? Life must be very fast there. How much do you earn? Do you get time to eat? If I come to Delhi, will you meet me?'

'Suppose I go to a five-star hotel in Bombay to have tea. How much will it cost me?'

I reply to his every question.

Finally, we rise to leave. I take out my wallet to pay for coffee, but like an elderly uncle, he holds my hand. 'No, you are my guest, I will pay. When I come to Delhi, then you pay,' he says.

We are at the entrance of the coffee shop. I ask him what he misses most. His eyes well up with tears. 'I miss my parents. When you are young, you get to learn so much from them. I couldn't do that,' he says.

We shake hands. As I turn away, two men wearing skullcaps and holding a large green cloth approach Vinod for alms. 'What is this for?' he asks.

'*Yateemon ke liye hein.*' This is for orphans.

Vinod takes out a fifty-rupee note and drops it into the cloth. And then I can no longer see his face. He walks towards the Secretariat.

A year and a half before the Wandhama massacre, seven Pandits were taken out of their homes and shot dead in Sangrampora. It was March 21, 1997. That night, Ashok Kumar Pandita slept early. In 1990, when the exodus happened, the Pandita family and a few others had decided to stay behind. The families depended on farming for their sustenance. During the day they tended to their fields. Often groups of militants would pass through their village. Ashok's old father was a wise man. He had one piece of advice to give to his son—No matter what happens, don't venture out of your house after sunset. That night, Ashok was woken up by a noise coming from downstairs. His aunt called out to him. But he remembered his father's advice and didn't venture out. She called out to him again. This time Ashok had to come out. The woman was worried about her son who had stepped out after hearing a noise. 'Go and see where Pyare Lal has gone,' she begged. Ashok came down and saw nine heavily armed men. They had brought with them four Pandit men from neighbouring houses. They had Pyare Lal as well. The men were carrying a list of names. 'Bring Avtar Krishen,' they demanded in chaste Kashmiri. Avtar Krishen was another cousin of Ashok's. On his walkie-talkie, they heard the chief of the militant group say, 'Major sahab, we are coming.'

One of the Pandits, Sanjay, started to plead with the militants. 'Please leave us; we have small children. What have we done?' he begged. One of the militants hit him with his gun and shouted, 'Don't try to be clever. Just keep your mouth shut.'

Then, led in a line by the militants, the men were made to walk a mile or so. At one spot, they were asked to remove their clothes. It had begun to drizzle. Ashok Pandita kept his watch. It had been gifted to him by his father. Then Avtar Krishen spoke up. 'What is our fault? We have always stayed here; we did not leave for Jammu. Why are you doing this to us?' he asked.

The militant abused him. 'Who asked you to live here, you infidels!' The Pandits began to cry. The militants cocked their rifles and began shooting. Eight men fell. The blood from their bodies mingled with rainwater to turn into pink puddles. Before they disappeared, the militants kicked the bodies to check if anyone was still breathing. They missed Ashok Pandita. He had been shot in the leg and had held his breath as he lay with his relatives, now dead.

In Habba Kadal, Sanjay Tickoo has lived with his family for the last two decades. Over the last few years, Tickoo and some of his friends who live in the Valley have been compiling a list of every Pandit who died in the nineties at the hands of militants. 'But not only that, every Pandit who died due to sunstroke or a snakebite is also a casualty of war,' he told me when I visited him at his house. Tickoo has also been instrumental in chronicling the damage to hundreds of temples and it is due to the efforts of his organization, the Kashmiri Pandit Sangharsh Samiti, that many temples have been renovated and attempts to sell temple land at various places have been thwarted.

On the morning of March 24, 2003, when Tickoo woke up, his wife told him that something had happened in Nadimarg village in south Kashmir. His wife's parents lived in a nearby village and she feared for their safety. Tickoo left immediately for the village with one of his friends. The scene when they arrived was grisly. Twenty-four Pandits, including women and children, had been shot dead by militants, helped allegedly by a party of local policemen. The previous night, the Pandits had been made to sit on the floor in a courtyard and shot in their heads.

I remembered speaking to one of the survivors, Mohan Bhat, many years ago in Jammu. He had lost his entire family to the massacre. He told me how the militants had shot a toddler who was crying.

'I was numb when I saw those bodies,' Tickoo told me. He composed himself, and asked his friend to hold a bowl of water. One by one, he lifted the shrouds from the faces of the dead, and as per Hindu rituals, put water in their mouths with a spoon. His friend, who was holding the bowl, ran away after Tickoo lifted the shroud off the third body. He couldn't bear it any longer.

Later, Tickoo asked a doctor to bandage the heads of the dead. And over that bandage he drew their features—eyes, nose, mouth, and ears—with vermilion paste. And then the bodies were consigned to the flames.

It is the spring of 2012. Shivratri is two days away. Every year, my father visits INA market in Delhi to buy puja paraphernalia. This year I tell him that I will buy it myself. I carry with me an empty rucksack to fill things in. I buy everything on the list father has prepared, and take the metro to return home. No sooner have I entered the coach than I start feeling uneasy. My heartbeat goes berserk, and there is a strange tingling sensation in my arms. I feel a sudden rush of heat in my stomach and I am dizzy. I get off at the next station. I put my bag down and slowly sink to the stairs. Ten minutes later I feel better. What happened to me? I ask myself. Was it a heart attack? But how can it be? I am physically fit. On reporting assignments deep in the jungles of central India, I walk for hours without any complaint. I do intense cycling over the weekends. I pick up my bag, slowly climbing the stairs to the main road, and call a friend who is a doctor and whose clinic is not far from where I am. It shouldn't take me more than twenty minutes to reach him.

I get into an auto rickshaw. We have hardly covered a mile when an attack strikes me again. This time it is more severe. I think I am becoming disoriented. I can barely keep my eyes open. Am I collapsing? With great difficulty, I manage to tell the driver that there is not enough time to reach the clinic. I ask him to take me to the emergency room in Moolchand hospital, only a mile or so away. I also think I should inform someone. But who? I have many friends, but somehow I cannot think of anyone whom I can call. Something feels so tangled inside me. We are stuck in a traffic jam and I am collapsing. I remember the driver looking at me in his rear-view mirror, crossing over on to the wrong side of the road and driving me to the hospital. Just before I enter, I call up a friend whose office is nearby. Then I calmly keep my bag in one corner of the emergency room and lie down on an empty bed.

Within minutes, all kinds of wires are strapped on to my chest. My finger is attached to a monitor, and someone inserts a needle in the back of my hand. I remember the back of my father's hand where an Om is tattooed. Someone takes a blood sample. A nurse tries to put an oxygen mask that I refuse. An electrocardiogram is taken, and my blood pressure is checked. Everything is normal. 'Probably an episode of hyperacidity,' the doctor says.

But I am shaken. I am not afraid of death. But I think of my father. What would he do if I were to die? The thought makes me shiver. I could die right now, I think, and nobody would be around to even hold my hand. I look over to my left; a man is puking blood. My friend still hasn't turned up. I close my eyes. I picture grandfather reciting the *Durgasaptashati*. I recite it in my head. I begin to feel calm. Suddenly nothing matters. I am ready to face anything.

After another electrocardiogram, the doctor says I can go home. 'Has his admit card been made?' she asks a nurse. 'We are waiting for his attendant,' she replies. I get up.

'It's ok, I will get it made,' I say. I pick up my bag. The collard greens will be ruined if they are not refrigerated soon. I walk to the reception, get myself admitted on paper, and fifteen minutes later, I am out of the hospital. I call a cab and go home. I manage to save the collard greens.

The attendant might not turn up. A man might indeed be an island. But as long as he remembers what his grandfather taught him, he will be fine.

Just before the winter in the Valley becomes unbearable for someone whose bones are now used to the heat of the plains, I want to make one trip there. But before that I must visit Jammu. I haven't been to the refugee camps in years. Moreover, in 2011, the camps were dismantled and their inhabitants shifted to a refugee settlement on the outskirts of Jammu city. The news from there is heartbreaking. The settlement is facing acute power and water shortages. The relief money offered to non-salaried refugee families has not been increased for years. Friends call from Jammu; a few camp residents are on a hunger strike.

I decide to visit Jammu first; from there I will go on to Kashmir. A few hundred Pandits have returned to the Valley under Prime Minister Manmohan Singh's 2008 resettlement package. What has been their experience so far? Also, I need to escape from Delhi for a while. Sometimes it closes in on me. It is then that I need to return home, to get a grip on life.

I call up Ali Mohammed. '*Khodayas path, sochan osus phone karay*—I swear by Allah, I was thinking of calling you,' he says.

'I'm coming.'

'That's the best thing you've done in months,' he says, and both of us laugh loudly.

There is another reason why I want to visit Kashmir this time. There is one thorn I need to take care of. I have visited Kashmir many times, and each time I have wanted to do this. I want to meet Irshad. After Ravi's death, we have had no contact with him. He has never visited us, never called us; nothing. Did he not want to know what happened to us, to Ravi's family, after his death? I have spoken to friends; they have found out that he teaches botany at the Kashmir University. This time I will meet Irshad.

'This summer so many people died,' said Bhushan Lal Bhat. 'In the afternoon you are fanning yourself as there is no electricity, and suddenly you hear a wail rising from a neighbouring flat,' he says.

We were sitting in Bhat's one-room set in Jagti Township, the new refugee settlement. The inhabitants, Bhat told me, refer to it as Jagti *Taavanship* (Jagti Hellhole). Situated twelve kilometres away from Jammu, about four thousand Pandit families shifted here from four refugee settlements in 2011. After the initial days of living in tents in the camps, the government constructed asbestos-roofed brick structures for the refugees to live in. The condition in these camps was pathetic. Now, the government was promising them a much better life in Jagti Township. And the camp inmates fell for the bait.

Bhat remembered his first few days in the quarter allotted to him. It rained one day and water seeped into his room from the balcony because of improper floor levelling. In no time, streamlets came gushing into his room from the leaking roof. 'I tried plugging in my television but the socket wouldn't work. When I opened it up, I found that there was no wiring,' said Bhat.

The families soon realized that they had been cut off from the city. Many families depended on the monthly relief of Rs 1,250 per head (not exceeding Rs 5,000 per family). When they lived in Jammu City, many men had taken on small private jobs to augment their income. But living in Jagti, these jobs became financially unviable. 'If I have to pay half my salary for transport then what do I bring home?' a man told me later. He had been working as a shop assistant in Jammu City, but now that he lived in Jagti, it was no longer feasible for him to keep his job. Also, many families had started small businesses, like grocery shops, in the old refugee camps. That income was gone as well since the shops promised to them in Jagti were yet to materialize. The worst affected were the children, who spent hours commuting to Jammu to attend school or tuitions.

There is no provision for sewage disposal in the settlement. The bodies of those who die have to be taken to Jammu since there is no provision for a cremation ground here. No transport is available after 8 p.m., and the road is so bad and deserted that women who are returning from the city often ask their male relatives to come and escort them. There has been no construction work for eight months at the site of a proposed hospital. Since the refugees did not have to pay for electricity in the old camps, they refuse to pay for electricity in Jagti. The township faces a daily power outage of sixteen hours; sometimes more. There is no electricity from 10.30 p.m. till 7 a.m.

Dr Ajay Chrungoo, one of the leaders of the Pandit political organization, Panun Kashmir, which has been demanding a

separate homeland for the Pandit community with Union
Territory status, told me that the refugees realized the folly of
shifting to Jagti. But it was too late to do anything. 'Immediately
after shifting people to Jagti, the government dismantled the
old camps. Had we protested they would have asked us to shift
back to tents,' he said.

Throughout the period of our exile, successive state
governments in Kashmir employed a novel way of thwarting
any allegation that they were biased against the Pandit
community. They would appoint a Pandit to the post of Relief
Commissioner. This fellow would always be more than keen to
follow diktats. One such officer, who was the Relief
Commissioner till February 2012, created a small lobby of
refugees in the camps who acted like his gendarmes in return
for small benefits. Those who tried to raise their voices against
inadequate facilities would have their ration cards scrutinized.
Even if one had a genuine ration card, the scrutiny took months,
during which the person's rights to claim relief money were
suspended.

Over the next few days, I spoke to dozens of people at the
Jagti Township. There were serious allegations that a major
chunk of the Rs 369-crore fund allotted for the township had
been siphoned off by various players. Independent tests
conducted on building material revealed that the ratio of cement
to sand in the plaster was less than half the normal ratio.
Instead of the standard three-layer water proofing, only a single
layer had been done. Electrical appliances and sanitary fittings
were of substandard quality. Most of the allegations seemed to
be true since within a year, the buildings developed cracks and
suffered water seepage. 'These buildings look like they were
built twenty years ago,' said Bhushan Lal Bhat.

I tried sending a list of questions to the Hyderabad-based Rithwik Projects Ltd, the company that was given the contract for building the township. The company's website had been suspended said a message on the site's homepage. Later it got running again. An email sent to its director, C.S. Bansal, bounced back. Repeated phone calls elicited no response.

That there had been a mass bungling in funds was also evident from the fact that the water plant at the township, built at a cost of eighteen crore rupees, has been non-functional from day one. So, most days, the township residents are left without water. At the height of summer, there has been no water for weeks. The management of the water plant was given to a private company, Sai Constructions, but they haven't been able to run it. In July 2012, the state Public Health Engineering and Irrigation Minister, Taj Mohiuddin, had to accept in the assembly that the water plant has been a failure. Out of desperation, many families have dug their own bore wells but the soak pits are two feet shallower than the required average height, resulting in the mixing of sewage with water.

I visited the office of the Relief Commissioner, which is situated near the canal. In one corner, a few Pandit refugees sat on strike to press for an increase in the monthly relief. The recently appointed Relief Commissioner, R.K. Pandita, was yet to arrive. A queue had already formed outside his office. Old men and women stood outside the closed door, perspiring, holding sheaves of documents in their hands. I saw a young girl standing there as well. An old man asked her what she had come for. 'For some personal work,' she replied. After a while, Pandita arrived in his official car and bolted inside his office. I waited for my turn to enter. The young girl's turn came before mine. From behind the closed door I heard her crying. Pandita was trying to console her. But I couldn't hear the reason for her tears. After five minutes or so, she came out. I stopped her and asked her to wait till I was done. She nodded.

Inside, in the middle of the room, R.K. Pandita sat listening to a woman who wanted a job for her son. No chairs had been placed in front of his desk. This, I guessed, was to make sure that nobody could relax and take longer than a few minutes to narrate their cup of woes. I sat on a chair placed in a corner. When the room was empty, I pulled my chair in front of the Commissioner.

Pandita told me that he had recently been appointed as the Relief Commissioner and was trying his best to make life easy for the Pandit refugees. 'You see, I am a refugee myself, then a Pandit, and then the Relief Commissioner as well. It is my duty three times over to ensure the welfare of the Pandits. But they need to start paying their electricity bills,' he said.

That evening, I returned to Jagti and shared this with Bhushan Lal Bhat. Since the news of the lack of power in Jagti had been making the rounds, a few young men from Kashmir, who are on Twitter, had been pointing out that many among those who refused to pay electricity bills in Jagti had been using air conditioners. I mentioned this to Bhushan Lal Bhat, who heard me out and took a deep puff from his Capstan cigarette. 'You see that,' he pointed to a picture of a Shivling on his wall, 'that used to be an old temple in my village in Pahalgam; after our exodus the militants blasted it. Tell me,' he continued, 'if my child is preparing for his engineering or medical entrance exam, and for his comfort I have installed a 0.8 ton AC, does that make me rich? I have to live and show my children that the world has not come to an end; we will live and prosper again, and we will rebuild our temples. What will make them (the government) happy? That we stand on the road and start begging for alms?'

Bhat may have installed an air conditioner. But I knew from visits to numerous other quarters in Jagti that many were leading a very difficult life. Rajinder Kumar Pandita was sleeping when I visited him. His wife was fanning him since there was no electricity, while his four daughters sat nearby. In the refugee camp, he had run a small shop and worked as a typist in a court. After he came to Jagti, he had to forego his shop and his job. He developed a kidney infection and suffered from high blood pressure. He was advised not to do any hard work or venture out in the heat. A few years ago, he had taken a loan of fifty thousand rupees towards which he was paying a monthly instalment of thirteen hundred rupees. So, out of the relief money of five thousand rupees, he had only thirty seven hundred rupees with which to feed six mouths. Each family member lived on twenty rupees a day, which is even lower than the Planning Commission's ridiculous definition of poverty. 'Tell me,' he said, 'how do I even send my children to school?'

Often, Bhushan Lal Bhat told me, impoverished families would come to him, requesting him to give them a handful of grain or some fruits. He did what he could, dipping in to the small supply he kept aside to offer to a priest on his father's death anniversary. Many, he said, reeled under heavy debt. Outside, old men playing cards spoke in hushed tones about a man who kept his front door locked and slipped in late at night through a window to escape the wrath of money lenders. Bhat said his business had failed.

'This is worse than the first exodus,' Ajay Chrungoo said.

When I land in Srinagar, Ali Mohammed is waiting outside the airport. He hugs me and takes my bag. 'It has been raining for days, but today it is sunny. You've brought the summer with you from Delhi.' I sit next to him. He takes out a pack of cigarettes, and I take one. We both smoke silently. From the Ram Bagh bridge, we turn left. I know he knows, but I tell him anyway. 'If we turn right, I will reach home.' He just nods. We pass by the Iqbal Park and the Bakshi Stadium where a farce of a parade is held every Independence Day and Republic Day. It is early afternoon and I think of going straight to the university after dropping my bag off at the hotel. The academic session is on at the university and I will find Irshad there.

I haven't been to the university in two years. The last time I was there, I was following a huge crowd of protestors agitating at the death of a teenage boy in a police firing. As the police charged at the crowd I took refuge inside the university. After a few minutes I came out only to be chased by a police vehicle down a street where I was pulled into a house by a helpful boy who was also a stone-pelting veteran. He looked at me, smiled and said, '*Bacch gaye!*' I was offered water and an invitation to the attic from where the action on the road was visible.

I remember coming out of the house and returning to a spot near the university gate. A boy rushed across the street. He had been hit on his head by a stone and blood was fast spreading over the rabbit on his Playboy T-shirt. There was teargas smoke all around. A magistrate wearing a cricket helmet stood at the gate. 'I don't know when this will end,' he said.

I remember walking with him for a short distance. A man in shabby clothes passed by us. The magistrate tried to stop him. 'Ashfaq, it is me,' he said. Ashfaq looked at him blankly, mumbled something and ran away. 'Allah!' the magistrate sighed. 'Can

you imagine? This man has a PhD, and now I don't know what
has happened to him.'

Meanwhile more teargas shells were being fired at the
protestors. At one end of the road, a constable holding a
transparent shield with 'Sexy Ayoub' scribbled on it, smoked a
cigarette. Without looking at me he said—'This teargas smoke
doesn't bother me any longer; even my tears have dried up.'

A little later, another police party made an appearance. The
protestors had been chased away. A paramilitary soldier walked
past a fallen motorcycle and smashed its rear-view mirror with a
blow of his lathi. 'They might turn on us now,' whispered a
fellow journalist, a Kashmiri, who had experienced this many
times in the past. Another policeman walked by, a little edgy.
'Are you from Delhi?' he asked me; and for lack of better words,
or perhaps just overwhelmed by emotion, he muttered—
'*Mohabbat aur jung mein sab jaayaz hai!*' (All is fair in love
and war).

And now I am back at the university, looking for an old friend
of Ravi's. The botany department is at the end of the road that
leads from the university's main gate. I enter. There is a garden
outside. On the ground floor is the zoology department. In the
main hall animal species lie preserved in formaldehyde in large
glass jars. I climb the stairs to the first floor and walk down a
corridor. At the end is a room outside which hangs Irshad's
name and designation. It is locked. There are two classes in
progress in adjoining halls. The doors are half open. I peep in.
But he is not there. A student walks by. 'Do you know where I
can find Dr Irshad?' 'He must be busy with the Science Congress,'
he replies. Science Congress! 'Do you have his number? I've
come from Delhi.' He doesn't have it. But he gets me the
number from another student. I call.

'Dr Irshad?'

'Yes?'

'Hi, where are you? I just wanted to meet you.'

He doesn't ask me who I am.

'Oh, I am busy. But I'll be there tomorrow; why don't you come tomorrow?'

I should tell him now.

'I have come from Delhi to see you. You wouldn't know who I am. I am Rahul. Rahul: Ravi's brother.'

'Oh!'

There is silence. 'Why don't you come tomorrow?' he asks.

'Ok, I'll come tomorrow.'

'Till when are you here?'

'I will be around for a few days.'

'Oh, in that case come any time. I will be at the university.'

The next day I cannot go to meet Irshad. I have to go to Vessu, in south Kashmir, where a few Pandits who returned at the government's behest live. In 2008, Prime Minister Manmohan Singh inaugurated the country's longest cantilever bridge in Akhnoor in the Jammu region, spanning the banks of the Chenab River. It was while standing on this engineering marvel that he announced a Rs 1,618-crore package to facilitate the return of the Kashmiri Pandits to the Valley. But no one quite understood why the Prime Minister had chosen Akhnoor to make the announcement. He should have either made it in a refugee settlement or in Srinagar. Many said it was to drive a wedge between the Pandit refugees of the 1990 exodus and those who had fled in 1947 from what is now Pakistan-occupied Kashmir to take refuge in Akhnoor and other border areas. Obviously, his advisors had not advised the Prime Minister well.

As a part of the Prime Minister's package, six thousand jobs were also announced for the Pandit youth in the Valley. But because of the fear of being targeted by militant and radical elements in Kashmir, most of these jobs were never filled. However, 1,446 applicants, many of them women who badly needed jobs, took up the offer. They were accommodated in five settlements across the Valley. Most of the jobs offered were as teaching staff in various government schools. Hoping for the best, these candidates shifted to the Valley. One of these five settlements is in Vessu, near Qazigund, on the Srinagar–Jammu highway. About seven hundred employees live there in cheap, single-bedroom, pre-fabricated structures. One such structure is shared by four employees. There is a very small kitchen and all four have to cook their meals there. There is no drinking water facility. The water supply is erratic, provided by tankers, and the residents boil that water for drinking. Otherwise, they go to a burst water pipeline nearby and collect water. The tanker water is so dirty, the few water purifiers the residents had have gone bust. The water situation is so bad that a day before I visited them, the residents blocked the national highway in protest. The previous December, after the schools closed for winter vacations, only a few non-teaching employees were left in the settlement. For the next three months, they had to melt snow on stoves for water. There was no electricity at all.

But the lack of basic amenities in the camp is the least of the inhabitants' concerns. The real problem arises, they said, at their workplaces where they face acute harassment from their Muslim colleagues. 'They treat us like pariahs,' said one female teacher. 'My headmistress threw a notebook at me the other day and shouted, "You sixth-grade pass-outs have come now to lord over us!" I wanted to tell her that I have a double Master's and a B.Ed degree.' Many in Kashmir clearly resented the return of Pandit employees under the package. 'When I ask for leave to go and visit my family in Jammu, my school in-charge does not respond at all,' said another Vessu camp resident. Many women face harassment while commuting to their workplace. 'I have been pinched so many times on the bus. You are standing in the bus holding the railing when someone comes and keeps his hand over yours. Or someone shouts menacingly, ordering you to keep your dupatta over your head,' said a female resident. 'Two of us were in the marketplace the other day when two men came up to us and commented that we were worth three lakh rupees,' recalled another.

These troubles have led to serious health issues among many. At least two female employees had to be admitted to the Qazigund hospital after they complained of chest pains and their blood pressure shot up. 'We are so depressed, I think most of us will leave these jobs in the coming months,' said another resident. 'Many women come to me in the middle of the night saying they can't sleep,' said a resident medical practitioner. 'All of them are on blood pressure lowering tablets.'

But leaving their jobs is not easy. Most of those who opted for them are in dire financial straits. 'The only other source of income is the five thousand rupee relief my family gets in Jammu. I have two children and this money is not even enough for their tuition fees. Now tell me, what do I do?' asked a resident.

Some have brought their children with them. But over the years, many schools, particularly in the rural areas, have switched over to a curriculum that focuses on religion. 'I put my son in the best school here, but they teach mathematics only twice a week. There is too much focus on Islamic studies; on studying the Koran,' said a resident.

But at least inside the settlement they are relatively safe. One woman employee chose to live outside the settlement in Pulwama with one of her erstwhile neighbours. Her father stayed with her as well. One late afternoon, while returning home, she was followed by four men in a car. 'Come, we will drop you home,' said one of them. When she refused politely, another told her, 'Look, I've not been able to sleep since the day I set my eyes on you. Let's marry, let's conduct a nikaah.' The woman left her job and returned to Jammu.

Many Pandit employees told me that they did not even receive their salaries on time. 'I have not received my salary for two months,' said one. In Baramulla in September, after an Indian cricketer scored a century, stones were pelted at the Pandit settlement there.

The Centre-appointed interlocutor on Jammu and Kashmir, Radha Kumar, once came to visit one of the camps. The women employees met her in private and narrated their woes to her. She reportedly told them that she had taught in Jamia (Jamia Millia Islamia University) for many years and that '. . . you have to learn to ignore such unpleasant experiences [of harassment at work places].' Some of the affected women had written to political leaders including the UPA chairperson Sonia Gandhi, requesting them to facilitate their transfer to Jammu. One such letter said—

> There is a freedom deficit which all of us are experiencing daily. We have been many times communicated indirectly that our speaking out the truth will bring trouble to us. In this atmosphere many of us chose to keep our experiences to ourselves. We do not have the adequate

confidence in the local administration because we are not sure of their maintaining strict confidentiality.

'Each day we leave behind something of our identity,' one woman said. 'Yesterday, it was the freedom to sing the National Anthem; today it is the freedom to wear a bindi; tomorrow it could be our faith.' She broke into sobs.

They all sat close to each other, on a thin rug, and soon others begin to weep as well. The women feel relatively safe inside the camp; outside, the world has changed. It is no longer the Kashmir it once was. 'When we became refugees in 1990, our lives became restricted to eight-by-eight feet rooms. More than twenty years later, we are still stuck,' said another woman. Her mobile rang. Her ring tone was the Gayatri Mantra. She picked up her phone, looked at the number flashing on the screen and mumbled, 'When I am out, I put my mobile on vibration mode.'

Later, I also visited the Sheikhpora Pandit settlement in central Kashmir, where some miscreants had recently thrown a carcass of a calf killed apparently by jackals. In August 2012, the residents of the settlement received a threatening letter sent by 'Jaish-e-Mohammed', triggering the fear of another exodus. The police dismissed the letter as a prank. The settlement is home to forty Pandit families who fled from various places in the Valley due to security issues. Many employees who returned under the Prime Minister's package live there as well. Though the building structures are much better than those in other settlements, issues of safety remain. 'I have asked them (the residents) to take even small signals of trouble very seriously,' Sanjay Tickoo told me later. In many ways, these settlements are ghettoes. And the lives of many Pandit residents are restricted by the boundary walls. In Sheikhpora, a woman who has been living there for seven years says she has been out of the settlement only thrice—once to visit her relatives in Jammu, and twice to visit the Kshir Bhawani shrine.

'*Dil chhum fatnas aamut*—my heart is about to burst,' she said.

The next day I call Irshad.

'Yes, I am here,' he says.

'Ok, I am coming.'

'Where are you?'

'I am near Lal Chowk. It should take me thirty or forty minutes to reach.'

In thirty minutes, I am at the gate of the University. In another five, I am climbing the stairs past the large glass jars. I walk down the corridor. Irshad's room is locked. He must be around. I wait. I walk up and down the corridor. Maybe he is teaching a class. But the classrooms are empty. Moreover, he would have told me if he had a class. I decide to call him. The phone rings but he does not answer.

I sit on a small bench. I wait. I look at the large board hanging at the entrance of the department. His name is there next to the subject he teaches: Ecological Botany and Reproductive Biology. I read other names as well. *He will come.* Biosystematics. *He must be around.* Biological Invasions and Biodiversity. *Maybe he is stuck somewhere.* Cytogenetics and Plant Breeding. *He will surely meet me.* Plant Pathology and Nematology. I call again. No response. The last time I call, he disconnects the call. It is clear: he does not want to see me.

I don't know why it is here that I am reminded of the young girl I had met at the Relief Commissioner's office in Jammu.

When I came out of his office, she was waiting outside. 'What happened, why were you crying?' I asked her. She told me her name was Supriya Bhat and she was studying in class eleven (so she was roughly the same age as I was when the exodus happened, I thought). She said she lived in the Jagti Township and each morning she took a bus to her school with her younger brother. A few days ago, the driver had suddenly applied the brakes due to which her brother's head banged against the windowpane. 'The driver scolded my brother badly. We pay him two hundred and fifty rupees per month for each student,' she said. I asked her why she had come to the Relief Commissioner's office. 'I came to request him to reprimand the driver,' she said. 'Value should be given to life, not materialistic things.'

Oh yes, child, value should indeed be given to life. I am overjoyed. May be our story will not come to an end in the next few decades. Maybe some of us will still be nicknamed Sartre. And did you notice, I am saying to myself, how perfect Supriya's elocution was? How assured her command over English? And Hindi? She spoke in Hindi as well. There was no problem of 'ba' and 'bha', 'ga' and 'gha'. She was so confident. God, she was so bright. God bless you, Supriya Bhat.

I also remember how I felt during a theatre performance, where two friends recounted the story of the celebrated Urdu writer, Saadat Hasan Manto, whose forefathers were Kashmiri Pandits. One of them quoted a line used by Manto's contemporary Krishan Chander to describe him—

By virtue of his disposition, temperament, features and his spirit, Manto remains a Kashmiri Pandit.

Hearing this buoyed me so much, I felt like whistling the way the front row audience sometimes whistled in a cinema hall.

And so, at the Kashmir University, I take out my notebook and write a short note. I hand it over to a lady in the administration department next to Irshad's room. 'Please give this to Dr Irshad,' I tell her. Then I leave.

'Chacha, cigarette,' I ask Ali Mohammed. '*Aish karith*—with pleasure,' he says.

Dear Irshad Bhai,

It seems we were not destined to meet this time. I came here on a personal journey, to walk through the corridors where many years ago you and Ravi must have walked together, brimming with youth and dreams of the future. Maybe if the catastrophe of 1990 had not struck us, you would still be together, perhaps teaching in the same department both of you graduated from. It makes me so happy watching young men and women in your department, looking at notice boards, carrying charts, and bent over their microscopes. It also gives me immense pleasure to see your name displayed so prominently on the staff list, along with your qualification and designation, and the subjects you teach. I wish all of your students the best for the future, and I wish you all good luck.

I will come again. I promise there will come a time when I will return permanently.

Yours,
Rahul (Ravi's brother)

. . . I will return permanently. I don't write it. That I say to him in my head.

TIMELINE

1846: Kashmir is bought from British colonialists by the Dogra Maharaja Gulab Singh who adds it to Jammu and Ladakh region to form the state of Jammu and Kashmir.

1931: Mass uprising against the Dogra Maharaja Hari Singh. A mob of the majority Muslim community targets the minority Hindus, known as Kashmiri Pandits. Property destroyed, several killed.

August 1947: India attains independence. Partition takes place, Pakistan is formed. Maharaja Hari Singh is still undecided about Kashmir's accession to either India or Pakistan.

October 1947: Aided by Pakistani army regulars, tribesmen from Pakistan's Northwest Frontier Province attack Kashmir in a bid to occupy it. Hundreds of Pandits and Sikhs are killed, and their women raped and taken as slaves to Pakistan. Thousands are forcibly converted to Islam. Pandit families living in border towns are forced to flee and take shelter in Srinagar and elsewhere.

Maharaja Hari Singh signs the instrument of accession with India. The Indian Army lands in Srinagar and the tribesmen are pushed back.

In the 1941 census, Kashmiri Pandits constitute about 15% of the Kashmir Valley's population. By 1981, they are reduced to a mere 5%.

February 1986: Major anti-Pandit riots break out in south Kashmir's Anantnag area. Pandits are beaten up, their women raped and several houses and temples burnt down.

July 1988: Two low-intensity bomb blasts rock Srinagar.

September 1989: Pandit political activist, Tika Lal Taploo is shot dead by armed men outside his residence.

January 1990: Massive crowds assemble in mosques across valley, shouting anti-India, anti-Pandit slogans. The exodus of Kashmiri Pandits begins. In the next few months, hundreds of innocent Pandits are tortured, killed and raped. By the year-end, about 350,000 Pandits have escaped from the Valley and taken refuge in Jammu and elsewhere. Only a handful of them stay back.

March 1997: Terrorists drag out seven Kashmiri Pandits from their houses in Sangrampora village and gun them down.

January 1998: 23 Kashmiri Pandits, including women and children, shot in cold blood in Wandhama village.

March 2003: 24 Kashmiri Pandits, including infants, brutally shot dead in Nadimarg village.

2012: Thousands of Pandits still languish in refugee settlements. After more than two decades, the Kashmiri Pandit community has still not been able to return to their ancestral land. They are dispersed all over—from Jammu to Johannesburg.

ACKNOWLEDGEMENTS

My heartfelt gratitude, first of all, to Ramachandra Guha, who mentored this book in many ways and chose it for the New India Foundation Fellowship.

In Mumbai: to Anupama and Vidhu Vinod Chopra, for making me remember long-forgotten stories of Kashmir; and to Abhijat Joshi, the most humble storyteller I've ever known.

In London: to Meru and Patrick French, the first believers of this book.

In New York: to Heather Gail Quinn, for her unflinching support and friendship.

In Kashmir: to Dr T.N. Ganjoo, Sanjay Tickoo, Suhail Bukhari, Zubair Dar, and Ali Mohammed, the quintessential Kashmiri.

In Jammu: to Dr Ramesh Tamiri, who allowed me to dip into his brilliant research material; and to Anuradha Bhasin, for instant access to *Kashmir Times* archives.

In Delhi: to Dr Shashi Shekhar Toshkhani; and to Geetika and Rashneek Kher, and Aditya Raj Kaul and Pawan Durani, whose belief in the book remained unwavering even during the fiercest of ideological face-offs. To Vinayak Razdan, whose splendid blog 'Search Kashmir' triggered off so many memories of home. To Richa Sharma, for sending talismans for this book. To Ajay

Bhardwaj, whose film *Ek Minute ka Maun* kept me alive in Delhi in the beginning.

In Kasauli: to Preetie and Rajesh Dogar, Sherry and Rajinder Chopra, Ashima and Iknam Bath—friends as thick as thieves.

To Arundhathi Subramaniam, for faith that spreads like 'the hum of crickets'; and to Hartosh Singh Bal, who knows what this book means to me.

To my parents, Shanta and P.N. Pandita, who suffered innumerable hardships in exile for my sake; and to my dear sister, Bharti.

To Anubha Bhonsle, for Moleskine notebooks, and for patiently listening to so many stories so many times over.

And, lastly, to Sir V.S. Naipaul, for his eternal lines: '*The world is what it is; men who are nothing, who allow themselves to become nothing, have no place in it.*'